Living Arctic

D0061913

ff

LIVING ARCTIC

Hunters
of the Canadian North

Hugh Brody

faber and faber

LONDON · BOSTON

First published in 1987
by Faber and Faber Limited
3 Queen Square London WC1N 3AU
Reprinted in 1988

Photoset and printed in Great Britain by
Redwood Burn Limited, Trowbridge, Wiltshire
All rights reserved

British Library Cataloguing in Publication Data

Brody, Hugh
Living Arctic.
1. Ethnology—Canada, Northern   2. Canada,
Northern—Social life and customs
I. Title
306'.09719'9   F1090.5

ISBN 0–571–15096–9

Published in collaboration
with the **British Museum** and
Indigenous Survival International

I have sat down many times
and thought over the differences or the distinction
between my people's way of life and your way of life.
... Your way of life, down south as white people, is a way
of life I myself would not want to live. We are
people who are free to go hunting
every day.

Peter Green
Paulatuk

The grass and the trees are our flesh,
the animals are our flesh.

Susie Tutcho
Fort Franklin

We are saying we have the right
to determine our own lives. This right derives
from the fact that we were here first. We are saying
we are a distinct people, a nation of people, and we
must have a special right within Canada.
We are distinct in that it will not be an easy matter
for us to be brought into your system because we are different.
We have our own system, our own way of
life, our own cultures and traditions. We have our
own languages, our own laws,
and a system of justice.

Robert Andre
Arctic Red River

Contents

Acknowledgements

This book has grown from some fifteen years of work in many parts of Arctic and Subarctic Canada. Such work entails the greatest possible dependence on men and women whose generosity, support and patience seem to know no limits. The people's knowledge and their willingness to share it are the foundations of this, and many other, projects. Of the many who have helped I especially want to thank Simon Anaviapik, Thomas Hunter, Abalie Field, Joshua Obed, Lottie Aragutaina and their families.

Living Arctic has been made as much as written. And the assembly of its elements has depended on friends and colleagues. Heather Jarman worked tirelessly at every stage, on every element. Others whom I also wish to thank for their incisive and skilful contributions are Miranda Tufnell, Kevin Busswood, Anthony Barnett, Jonathan King, Nigel Parry, Georges Erasmus, Dave Monture, Cindy Gilday, Richard Overstall, Michael Jackson, Paul Wilkinson and Chris Nobbs.

Indigenous Survival International and the Ethnography Department of the British Museum, London, provided generous financial, logistical and moral support. Library staff at the Scott Polar Research Institute, Cambridge, were endlessly helpful with their knowledge of the literature and archives. The Department of Indian and Northern Affairs and the Secretary of State of Canada provided generous funding and kindly gave permission for me to use quotations from the Inuit Land Use and Occupancy Report.

Nonetheless, I am conscious that in a book of such wide historical and ethnographic scope, there are bound to be errors and weaknesses. Responsibility for these is mine.

A Note on the Photographs

Photographs allow a sudden and surreal intimacy. With almost no preparation, after the briefest of journeys, they parachute us into distant homes. We look into other people's faces, caught and frozen in exact likeness, a few feet from where we, the cameras, are placed. We are made to feel that no detail of hunting and trapping need escape us. A set of such photographs does not carry information so much as effortless proximity, a denial of distance. This is their appeal, their strange and special advantage. It is also their danger.

The black and white images in this book are placed to lead into the text, to be part of a journey that may justify the intimacy they offer. They are not illustrative in any narrow sense, nor are they representative. A disproportionate number are from the Arctic; far too few from the eastern Subarctic. This is not an intentional bias; it simply reflects photographers' preferences and chance. The photographs stand as evocations and symbols of *Living Arctic*'s argument.

The colour plate section in the middle of the book exists apart from any text. Here is the vividness, the glow of life in the north. We can move amid this life, in part as we might turn back and forth the pages of an atlas, in part as we read a poem. Some of what we see is clear and self-evident; some is embedded in glimpses of another world or juxtapositions of images that go beyond any possible caption.

The photographs come from many different sources. I especially want to thank Ulli Steltzer, Richard Harrington, Dan Orienti, Father Rene Fumoleau, Bryan and Cherry Alexander, Anne Cubitt, Father Guy-Mary Rousselière, John MacDonald, George Qulaut, Adrian Tanner, Nelson Graburn, Anita Hearle, Tessa Macintosh and the Northwest Territories Government, Jeanne L'Espérance and the Public Archives of Canada, the

xi

A Note on the Photographs

Notman Archives at McCord Museum of McGill University, Montreal, the Synod Archives of the Anglican Church of Canada, the National Museum of Canada, Ottawa, and Shirley Ann Smith and the Hudson's Bay Company Archives. All these people and institutions offered their work in support of Indigenous Survival International, the Living Arctic exhibition at the British Museum, and allowed use of their photographs in associated publications. Detailed credits are on pp. 243–8.

Preface

I write about the far north in the belief that we can best discover
who we are by going to what we think of as the margins of our
world. Faced with societies and lands that question our everyday
assumptions and challenge our preconceptions, it is possible to
discover both the importance of others and truths about ourselves.

Living Arctic is about a vast region for whose peoples – the
Inuit, Dene, Cree, Naskapi, Innu and Métis – it is a bountiful
and beautiful homeland. But this land has been claimed by newcomers. The peoples' histories, languages and wisdom have been
challenged; some of their resources expropriated. The newcomers disregard histories or turn them into folktales, impose
foreign languages and advocate new beliefs. To societies that
depend upon spiralling needs and accumulation of surplus, hunters appear to be simple and destitute.

Aboriginal peoples across the Canadian north say that
southerners' blindness to hunting and trapping cultures can only
be a result of too little knowledge. Despite unease about intrusive
outsiders, this means that the people support those who take the
time to get to know them on their own terms, and encourage
them to publicize the facts. So sure are the hunters and trappers
of the fundamental truth and rightness of their position that they
trust that anyone who knows them – be it southerners or their
own children – will be quite unable to misjudge, misrepresent or
wrong them. Upon knowledge, they insist, must the future be
built.

But the facts that I have compressed into the limited space of this
book do not quite speak for themselves. They are not neutral
pieces of information. Interest in other places is deeply comparative. We look at 'them' with reference to 'us'. Europeans have
often done this in order to note relative superiority. We see our-

selves as higher on the ladder of progress. Compared to other peoples and other times, we think of ourselves as secure, prosperous, wise, knowledgeable, artistic and leisured. And we believe the future belongs to us and our ways.

The trouble with the facts about tribal cultures in general and hunting cultures in particular is that they subvert any tendency we might have to think of them as inferior. Indeed, they invite another kind of comparison: who, in our society, has leisure, wealth and security? Who is shaping the future? Not the majority. And how do hunters' and trappers' lives compare with those among ourselves who are *not* privileged?

Answering these questions leads to an appreciation of northern hunting cultures that is not flattering to our own. It points towards the inequality as well as the uncertain prosperity of 'civilization'. And it adds to the reasons among the privileged for wanting to keep hunting peoples as representatives of the past.

To defend their homelands against misunderstanding and incursion the people have adopted many idioms. They speak of rights and jurisdictions; they argue for a distinctive place within nation states; they make use of new technologies and Christian beliefs. Hunters and trappers of the north do not defy the new simply with the old. They are not representatives of an ancient world that is slowly and painfully sinking beneath waves of modernity. Rather, they are our contemporaries. They have lived, learned and adapted for as many millennia as all other human beings. To contemplate their skills, material goods and ways of life, therefore, is to enjoy the privilege of a journey into the variety and complexity of human culture. But we must not mistake this for a journey through time: we are not contemplating, here, our own ancestry. However far we may go to find the hunters of the Canadian north, we remain in the present.

Here is the central difficulty. Celebration of the modernity of northern hunting cultures fits uneasily with anthropological writing and exhibitions. Labelled and displayed behind glass, inert and mute, museum exhibits seem to belong to some other time. Ethnographic details about other, distant cultures all too often seem to preserve that which would otherwise be lost only for a posterity of libraries. Even when we are told that objects are a part of modern life, they nonetheless acquire a strangeness, a fustiness. Removed from their living environment, artefacts on display appear as human taxidermy. They are appropriated by the visitor or reader; and they are diminished by being encompassed within a necessarily limited understanding. The modernity, vitality and real richness of cultures we may wish to celebrate are easily smothered. An essay or labels may describe the ways in which northern hunting peoples continue to live and to make their livings in their homelands, but in a museum this Arctic can all too easily be anything but alive.

How can we escape from this contradiction? How can an anthropological work or museum avoid antagonism between form and content? By what means can the quality of an exhibition or a publication accord with its intentions?

Living Arctic seeks to overcome the contradiction in two ways. First, the voices of the people must be heard; their words breathe life into our understanding. We cannot know other cultures by looking at them; we must hear their accents, absorb their intonations, and enter their points of view. In film, and even in an exhibition that uses sound, voices can be heard. But in writing, the best we can do is use the peoples' own statements – as a pathway through, and a frame within which to see, information.

Second, we must keep an argument at the centre of what is written. Briefly, this argument states that northern hunting peoples, like most aboriginal or tribal groups, have had to survive in defiance of a stereotype. Their ways of living and thinking are regarded as primitive, their wealth is characterized as poverty. This denies northern peoples their rights to land, challenges their freedom to hunt, fish and trap in ways of their own choosing; it questions parents' responsibilities for their own children, and obscures the viability of their ways of life. Again and again we must deal with the nature and consequences of these stereotypes.

Living Arctic attempts to describe life in a huge terrain. The Canadian Arctic and Subarctic spread across almost four million square miles, home to at least five aboriginal cultures. Justice cannot possibly be done to such immense ethnographic variety. But an advantage comes with generality. Hunters and trappers of the north share both a unique cultural form and a particular experience of modern history. At times, it will be important here to speak of one cultural group rather than another, of the Inuit as opposed to the Dene or Cree, the Innu as opposed to the Métis. More often, however, it is possible to speak and write of the people as a whole; the difference between them and us, rather than the myriad differences among themselves, is at the heart of this project.

The separations between the chapters of this book are artificial; the cultures themselves are holistic: complex links tie each element to the others. Hunters' mobility is inseparable from their reliance on meat, from their ways of bringing up children, from their languages, from their spirituality. The photographs and quotations from individuals across the north make some of the connections.

Much of the material, social and intellectual culture of northern hunters and trappers is threatened; some has been damaged and even lost. Their startling achievement, however, is resilience. Every family lives with and makes use of industrial culture, yet depends on the resources of the land, on hunting and trapping. For the most part, this book is written in the present tense.

Chapter 1

Stereotypes

... it is not to be called The new Land,
but rather stones and wilde cragges, and a place
fit for wilde beastes, for in all the North Iland I did not
see a cart-load of good earth: yet went I on shoare in the
many places, and in the Iland of White Sand, there is
nothing else but mosse and small thornes scattered here
and there, withered and dry. To be short, I beleeve
that this was the land that God
allotted to Caine.

Jacques Cartier, French mariner
Labrador, 1534

The land is so beautiful with its high rivers
and lakes waiting to be fished. It has great mountains,
and images form as if you could be
caribou among them.

Rosie Paulla
Gjoa Haven, 1976

These men may very well and truely be called Wilde,
because there is no poorer people in the world.
For I thinke all that they had together,
besides their boates and nets was not worth five souce.
They go altogether naked saving their privities,
which are covered with a little skinne,
and certaine olde skinnes
that they cast upon them.

Jacques Cartier
Labrador, 1534

3

Stereotypes

When I went to school in Fort McPherson
I can remember being taught that the Indians
were savages. We were violent, cruel and uncivilized.
I remember reading history books that glorified
the white man who slaughtered whole
nations of Indian people.
No one called the white men savages,
they were heroes who explored new horizons
or conquered new frontiers.

Richard Nerysoo
Fort McPherson, 1977

The Condition of these poor People
is melancholy enough, tho' it does not
make such an Impression on them as one would expect;
for tho' the best Part of their Life is spent in
procuring Necessaries for the subsistance of
themselves and of their Families; yet they
have no great Notion of Frugality, or
providing against those Distresses, to which
they are sure to be exposed every Winter, are very
free of their Provisions, when they
have plenty, and except drying a
little Venison and Fish, take no
Care for supplies, in a
time of Dearth.

Henry Ellis, agent on Dobbs Galley
1748

This land is just like our blood because we live
off the animals that feed off the land . . . We are not like
the white people. We worry about our land because we
make our living off our land. The white people they
live on money. That's why they worry
about money.

Louis Caesar
Fort Good Hope, 1977

... nothing short of persecution could have
driven them to take up their abode in these extreme
parts of the globe, amidst ice and snow,
where worse than Cimmerian darkness dwells for half
the year ... Theirs, it must be confessed, is a most cruel and
wretched lot, for whom any permanent relief
appears to be hopeless, surrounded as
they are in every part of the coast-land,
bounding the dreary
Polar Sea.

Sir John Barrow, Second Lord of the Admiralty
1846

This land of ours is
a good land and it is big, but to us Inuit
it is very small. There is not much room. It is our own
land and the animals are our own, and we used to be free
to kill them because they were our animals.
We cannot live anywhere else, we cannot drink
any other water. We cannot travel
by dog-teams in any other place
but our land.

Innakatsik
Baker Lake, 1974

Their lives are bereft of peace and comfort,
devoid of even the smallest reward ... Surely here
were the poorest of the poor,
physically and morally.

Father Roger P. Buliard, missionary
1953

It is very clear to me that it is an important
and special thing to be an Indian. Being an Indian
means being able to understand and live with this world in a
very special way. It means living with the land, with the animals,
with the birds and fish, as though they were your sisters and
brothers. It means saying the land is an old friend and an
old friend your father knew, your grandfather knew,
indeed your people always have known ... we see
our land as much, much more than the white
man sees it. To the Indian people
our land really is our life.

Richard Nerysoo
Fort McPherson, 1977

They gathered their food with the weapons of
the men of the Stone Age, they thought their simple,
primitive thoughts and lived their insecure and tense lives ...
archaeological remains found in various parts of the world
... tell a fascinating story to him whose scientific
imagination can piece it together and fill in the wide gaps;
but far better than such dreaming was my present
opportunity. I had nothing to imagine; I had merely to
look and listen; for here were not remains of the Stone
Age, but the Stone Age itself ...

Vilhjalmur Stefansson, explorer anthropologist
1913

We are not looking back.
We do not want to remain static.
We do not want to stop the clock of time.
Our old people, when they talk about how the Dene ways
should be kept by young people ...
they are not looking back, they are looking forward.
They are looking as far ahead into the future as
they possibly can. So are we all.

Georges Erasmus
Yellowknife, 1977

9

The voices of hunters and trappers of the far north have been raised in defiance of stereotypes that imply they are dying or have become exotic specimens within a museum of ancient history. These are people who insist on their distinctive and separate histories to show that they are equally human and properly entitled to their ways of life. They emphasize distinctiveness to reveal their equality. At the same time, the hunter's way of life is one of the most flexible and adaptive of human systems. They welcome and make use of new thoughts and foreign artefacts. This is revealed in the smallest details of their technology; it also explains the welcome they gave to the newcomers, and is implicit in the generous hospitality they showed them. Profound believers in equality, the hunters of the north express incredulity as well as dismay when they discover that their guests consider them to be lesser beings perched at an uncomfortable margin of the world.

Very few Europeans have been to the Arctic. It is a land without roads, has a tiny scattering of towns and the thinnest trickle of tourists. Neither has the Arctic come to us – in the way, for example, that the Orient has. We do not wear clothes made from Arctic fabrics. We do not eat Arctic foods. Very few Athapaskan, Algonquian or Eskimo words have entered the English language.* Furs, whale oil and whalebone have, of course, played their part in European history. The men who brought these goods to Europe have been celebrated as great adventurers and heroes. But even the voracious and catholic appetites of European culture have found little or nothing in Arctic cultures to absorb and make their own.

---

* The Athapaskan *uskadje* has turned into whisky jack, popular name for the Canada grey jay. The English words 'pekan', the name of a large North American marten, and 'toboggan' are of Algonquian origin. 'Kayak', 'anorak' and 'igloo' are all direct transliterations from the Eskimo language. 'Parka' comes from Aleut.

11

Nonetheless, the far north has been a focus of intense interest for at least four centuries. As imagery and metaphor, as challenge and menace, as romance and adventure, the Arctic worked as keenly on the European imagination as any other geographical region. How are we to explain this combination of distance and proximity, cultural separation and obsession?

The first part of an answer lies in the relationship between peasant and hunter. A second part takes us to the history of Arctic exploration and the search for the Northwest Passage.

The modern empires that now vie with one another for material and cultural domination of the world emphasize their historical and social differences. The rhetoric of global politics is replete with insistence by one or another of the superpowers that their institutions and points of view are underpinned by distinctive history and culture. Yet all these nations have in common one factor that provides a profound cultural unity – namely, an agricultural heritage. The commonality of social and mental form may be traced even more specifically to peasant forms of agriculture. This foundation of so many societies means that ideas about land, property, religion, sexuality, children, patriarchy and social control are also shared. Urban and suburban attitudes to hunters are still shaped by an agricultural and peasant history that bridges other ideological chasms.

Hunters do not share peasant and urban consciousness. Their ideas and institutions, their views about property, children, sexuality and social control, are radically unlike those founded in settled, originally agricultural societies. Peasant attachment to specific plots of land, the wish to have large numbers of children in short periods of time, emphasis upon marriage, subordination of women to men, preoccupation with private ownership, and bodies of explicit law that are enforced by some form of police – all these notions and practices are deeply alien to most hunting societies.

13

The gulf between hunter and peasant consciousness that is revealed by so many opposing ideas, ideals and social habits is reinforced, in the case of the hunters of the far north, by climate. In all peasant-originated systems, soil and warmth define a framework of wellbeing. Late frosts and early winters are the enemy. Cold is a symbol of lovelessness, poverty and fear. A world without summer becomes a world without the possibility of human existence.

For those of us who have been raised within a culture of soil, warmth and settled life, the geographical and social terrains of northern hunters constitute a startling, perhaps even terrifying, reversal of the human condition. This reversal presents a challenge. As an image of reality, the far north, and the life of the hunters in it, beckons with blandishments of pristine emptiness and the challenge of absolutely new opportunities. As both incentive and metaphor, this apparent reversal of the human condition makes powerful appeals to the imagination.

Preoccupation with the Arctic found an outlet in the enduring belief in, and search for, a Northwest Passage. This quest lasted for over four hundred years, from 1497 to 1905; it persisted in defiance of apparent proof repeated in each generation that no such route existed; it continued despite the loss of ships and men and money; it was justified to monarchs and private investors by a multitude of arguments and was supported by quoting Greek philosophers, supposed commercial good sense, fake maps, nationalistic ideals and scientific aims. The Northwest Passage was an obsession, whose acting out helped create the stereotype through which we Europeans view the north and its native peoples today.

In 1497, the Venetian sailor John Cabot convinced Henry VII that by sailing westward at high latitudes he could open up a short route to the Orient, which would, as Sir Humphrey Gilbert pointed out in 1576, 'be a great aduauncement to our Countrie, wonderfull inriching to our Prince, and unspeakeable commodi-

ties to all the inhabitants of Europe'.* Cabot failed to find a way through the North American continent, but for the next three centuries little enough was known about Arctic geography that each expedition could claim to have been looking in the wrong place and express the certainty that the next would succeed.

By the early nineteenth century, scientific aims had been added to commercial dreams, and the conclusion of the Napoleonic Wars left the Admiralty free to pursue urgings of the Royal Society for peacetime exploration. There followed a spate of expeditions: Ross in 1818 and 1829; Parry in 1819, 1821 and 1824; Lyon in 1824; Franklin overland in 1819 and 1825 and finally the 1845 voyage from which no one returned. These expeditions were often frozen in, and spent long winters in the Arctic far from other European company. Both to fulfil their scientific aims and to provide amusement for themselves, ships' officers entertained 'Natives' on board, visited their settlements and even learned a little of their languages. They recorded their observations at great length and illustrated them with detailed sketches.

The search for the Northwest Passage captured the popular imagination to such an extent that Mary Shelley's *Frankenstein*, published in 1818 in its original pre-Hollywood version, is set aboard a ship in Arctic waters, and expresses the romantic enthusiasm with which the British public greeted published versions of explorers' diaries. From these they gained their view of the hunters of the north.† Since the distance a ship from England could penetrate during the ice-free summer period usually left the explorers frozen into the territory of the Central Canadian

---

* Sir Humphrey Gilbert, *A Discourse Of a Discoverie for a new Passage to Cataia*, 1576.

† In the mid-nineteenth century, whaling ships brought Inuit to Europe, where they were put on display. For the most part, these visitors, many of whom died of European diseases, came from Greenland. They were exhibited as strange savages, and seem to have contributed far less to popular stereotypes than the explorers' writings.

Arctic, its people, especially the Iglulingmiut with their snow houses and dog sleds, became the Eskimo of our imagination. Parry's descriptions and Lyon's drawings were quoted and re-published frequently.

The Eskimo makes his and her appearance with a smile. Imposed on the stereotypical background of impossible terrain and intolerable weather is an eternally happy, optimistic little figure; a round, furry and cuddly human with a pet name; a man or woman who amazes and delights our European representatives with innocent simplicity. Gorge themselves as they might on raw meat and blubber, a stereotypical Eskimo of the impossible north wages his battle against environment in astonishingly good humour. Ironically, this stereotype of the Eskimo conforms to a puritanical ideal. In the farthest north, fatalism and an unremitting workload in the face of grim circumstances seem to be accepted with a cheerfulness that could be held up as a model to every factory worker in the newly industrial world.

By comparison, the stereotype of the Indian was shaped by the history of westward settlement in the United States and southern Canada. This led to a series of wars and disputes between white farmers and indigenous hunters, which were popularized (as well as caricatured) in the cowboys-and-Indians idiom. Very few northern hunters occupied lands with agricultural potential, but they have been endowed with danger by virtue of being labelled 'Indians'. The 'Eskimo' smiles from the sidelines; the 'Indian' is cunning, warlike and stands in our way. This distinction between the two peoples is a geographical and anthropological myth, but the double northern stereotype has nonetheless persisted.

The notoriety of the dangerous Indian was spread in the 1900s by American film studios' reliance on the 'western' formula. At the same time, the popularity of the smiling Eskimo was secured on a massive scale by the explorer-cum-film-maker Robert Flaherty. His *Nanook of the North* appeared in 1922. It

became the first documentary film of its kind to achieve worldwide box office success. *Nanook* was marketed as the irresistible hero of a Shakespearian love story, a man pitted against the most ferocious odds imaginable, brave, courageous and in some sense doomed by the tragedy intrinsic to a life in such a place. These were the themes worked by publicity writers and designers of *Nanook*'s advertisements. The appeal was made to fertile ground, and audiences crowded to see *Nanook* in virtually every cinema in the world. In Germany, Nanook ashtrays became popular bric-à-brac. Nanook ice creams were marketed in the United States. And when the hunter who played the part of Nanook died of starvation in the barrens, his death was mourned in China.

Flaherty's brilliance as a film-maker was compounded by the sharp simplicity of his theory of the film. His lifelong theme, in fact, became man against nature. Heroic simplicity against savage environment. *Nanook*'s popularity, therefore, is inseparable from the way in which the film plays upon and reinforces stereotypes of hunters. The images of *Nanook of the North* add to the accounts penned by explorers for the Northwest Passage: they paint a picture of simplicity and benighted impoverishment that northern peoples themselves, as well as the anthropologists who have lived amongst them, have to struggle to overthrow.

The smiling, innocent Eskimo; the savage, cunning Indian. The one at war with nature, the other with settlers. The stereotypes maroon northern hunting peoples in an intriguing but irrelevant past. To establish themselves as existing in the present, people of the north have to demonstrate again and again, in whatever way they have at their disposal, that their view of the world and their ways of life are as rich and modern as anyone else's.

Chapter 2

Peoples

*

Like all nations with ancient roots,
our culture has given reason to our world. Even with
so many new pressures, our style of government is unchanged,
the languages we speak are still our own. Our drums
bring us together as in the past. Our songs are still sung for
the happiness of a good day, in thanksgiving to
the Creator, or in prayerful supplication.

Denendeh, A Dene Celebration

Using that little pencil.
Hard going! Whites are amazing.
They do so much work that doesn't look like
work at all. And I thought, even if I learn
things at school, I'll never be
a real white man.

Paulussi Inukuluk
Pond Inlet

*

The Dene say that they have always lived on their ancestral territories. To them, movement and change occur on a huge map, over countless generations. Their oral histories make connections between the earliest moments of life, when animals and humans were inseparably joined, and the lands they still hunt and trap. In this way, hunters affirm the eternal link between culture and place.

Inuit stories, on the other hand, record their arrival in what is now Arctic Canada. And they tell of those whom their ancestors met – a strangely timorous people who ran away and disappeared. This difference between Dene and Inuit history is echoed by findings of modern science.

In the Arctic, the earliest archaeological sites have been dated to between 2500 BC and 2000 BC. They are known to archaeologists as Independence I and Pre-Dorset and later as the Dorset. Old house sites, bone and ivory harpoon heads, soapstone lamps, snow knives, tiny ivory carvings and the occasional remnant of a beautiful mask evoke a culture not dissimilar from historic Inuit. But between the eleventh and thirteenth centuries AD, the Thule culture – direct ancestors of today's Eskimoan peoples – arrived on the Arctic scene as the Dorset Culture was disappearing. And this is just what Inuit stories describe.

Archaeologists date the occupation of the central and eastern Subarctic to approximately 7500 BC. Evidence for this exists in scattered campsites with stone skin scrapers, arrow tips and blades. Given the thousands of years and tens of thousands of square miles with which archaeologists must deal, their record is built on tiny evocations, fractured hints of a stream of human life that made no records and left few marks. But archaeologists and the people agree that the Algonquian way of life has persisted on the lands where it now is found for at least 7000 years.

25

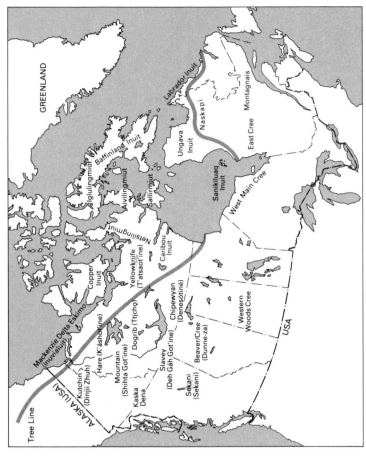

1. *The peoples of the Canadian north.*

The map shows the northern peoples identified by anthropologists. Dene groups have their Athapaskan names in brackets. The affix 'miut' is Eskimo for a social group. Placing of the names is approximate: there are many overlaps and historical changes in distribution, especially among Cree and Dene of the Subarctic.

In the western Subarctic, archaeologists trace Athapaskans only as far back as 500 BC. But in the corridors of land that opened as the glaciers of the last ice age receded, forerunners of today's Athapaskans left hints of their lives – small stone blades, hearths with remains of caribou bones, tools for shaping bone and wood. As early as 9000 BC, hunters in western Alaska were using stone tools that look similar to those in Asia. From this evidence, archaeologists say that northern North America was peopled by immigrants from Asia, coming over the land bridge that once connected Siberia with Alaska, or across the narrow stretch of ice or sea that is now the Bering Straits. And they say that the first of these immigrants may have hunted in Alaska and the Yukon Territory as long ago as 25,000 BC.

The connections made by modern science between the cultures of today and those who first lived in the far north are thus tenuous. Ancient peoples are indicated by prefixes of limited meaning: proto-Athapaskans, palaeo-Indians, pre-Dorset, palaeo-Eskimo.

From an archaeological point of view, the climate is an asset. The dry cold of the far north means that artefacts and human remains lie close to the surface and remain undecayed for an astonishingly long period. Tent rings, house sites and graves continue to break through the surface of the tundra for several centuries. Masks and harpoon heads dating back several thousands of years lie preserved in the permafrost less than a metre underground. Northern hunters, however, thrived by never stopping at any site for more than a fleeting moment of the archaeological timescale. And they enjoyed the advantages of technology that could be carried as much in the mind as on the back. They left little – however well preserved – for archaeologists to find. The things they made and on which they depended dissolved back into the land from which they had come.

Yet the little is enough to persuade archaeologists to agree

2. *The Inuit of north Baffin*

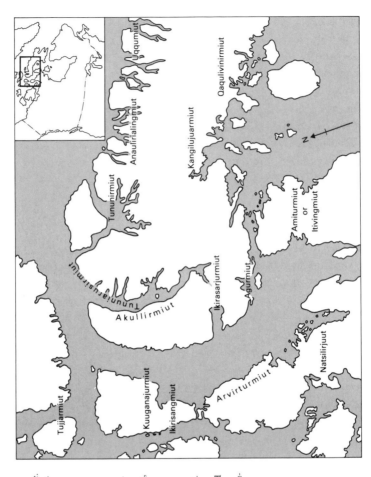

Agurmiut: The windward people. *Akullirmiut:* The middle people. *Amiturmiut:* People of the small region. *Anaulirialingmiut:* The fish-clubbing place people. *Arvirturmiut:* Bowhead whale-eating people. *Ikirasarjurmiut:* The small narrows people. *Itivingmiut:* People across the land. *Kangilujuarmiut:* Large inlet people. *Kuuganajurmiut:* The fast, large river people. *Natsilirjuut:* People where there are seals. *Qaquivinirmiut:* Snow goose remains place people. *Ikirisangmiut:* People of the narrows. *Tujjarmiut:* The rough ground place people. *Tununirusimiut:* Second shaded place people. *Tununirmiut:* Shaded place people. *Uqqumiut:* Lee side people.

source: *Inuit Land Use and Occupancy Project*, ed. Milton Freeman, Ottawa: Minister of Supply and Service, 1976.

with Dene oral tradition at least to the extent of saying that hunting peoples have lived in the far north whenever it was free of a year-round covering of ice. The tundra, scrub and grasslands at the glaciers' edges – perhaps even land fjords reaching deep into the ice – have provided a world in which hunters could thrive. Whenever and wherever they were able, human beings have chosen to live in the Arctic and Subarctic regions.

The mosaic of territories and societies in the Canadian north is far more elaborate than scientists' maps can reveal. The way the foot of a sealskin boot is patterned, the accent placed on words, the open area preferred for summer camping – with these kinds of detail people express differences among themselves. These are the living breath of culture, the facts that give pleasure and compel daily attention.

Anthropologists divide the peoples of northern Canada into three large groups: Athapaskans of the western Subarctic, Algonquians of the eastern Subarctic and Eskimoans of the Arctic. These groupings are linguistic – they correspond to three separate language families. Each group is made up of smaller groups of people – bands, tribes, nations – who live in discrete territories, have their own dialects and social and material cultures that are distinctive to European eyes. Thus, Athapaskans are divided into Dogrib, Hare, Kutchin, Dunne-za or Beaver, Slavey and others. Algonquians are split into Cree, Naskapi and Montagnais. Eskimoan groups include the Mackenzie or Inuvialuit, Copper, Netsilik, Caribou, Iglulik, Ungava and so on.

In many ways these anthropological groupings coincide with the peoples' own definitions. Most Athapaskans now call themselves Dene or Dena – a term or affix in their languages meaning people or humans. Algonquians in Labrador use their word for people, Innu, to refer to themselves. Eskimoan peoples of Canada call themselves Inuit, which also means persons or human beings. And within these large divisions are groups which, though most do not use the names newcomers have given

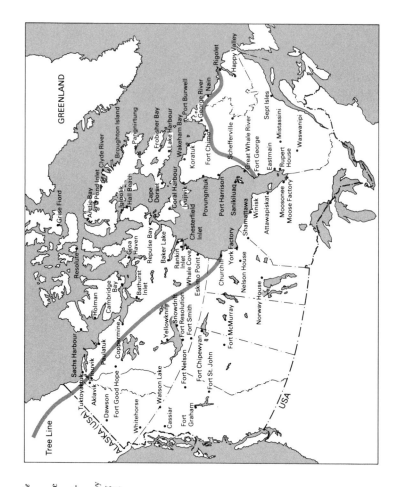

3. *Modern towns and villages of the Canadian north*

The hunters and trappers of the Canadian north now spend much of each year in communities for the most part set up by fur traders and then enlarged by government agencies. Hunting and trapping territories spread all around these places.

them, correspond to the boundaries marked on anthropological maps.

This book mainly uses the peoples' own names – Dene, Innu and Inuit. Occasionally smaller groupings are referred to by their anthropological labels. Often, however, the subject of this book is the hunters and trappers of the north, or simply the people. In relation to the forces that impinge upon their lives and threaten their lands, the many different groups of Arctic and Subarctic Canada have all too much in common.

The modern populations of Dene, Inuit, Innu and Métis (the descendants of alliances between Dene or Cree and white fur traders)* are scattered throughout the Canadian north. The principal villages and settlements can be mapped. But dots on a vast landscape are misleading. Hunting and trapping territories are not confined even to the immediate hinterlands of these modern villages. They spread across the land, often stretching into areas that lie far from centres set up by fur traders, missionaries and white administrators. Within each territory are camps, cabins and old village sites that constitute another level of residency that belies the isolation of little communities separated by vast tracts of seeming wilderness.

The entire land – including its lakes and sea ice – is known, named and invested with meaning by being used and managed by hunters and trappers. Icecaps and mountain peaks aside, there is no such thing as Arctic and Subarctic wilderness. The dotlike villages on maps show where people now live, where they have their modern addresses. But as families, societies and cultures, the peoples' collective home is the entire north.

---

* The Métis have always been most numerous and culturally distinct in mid-western Canada. An important group, however, live along the Mackenzie Valley. They ally themselves with the Dene of that region. For more detail of Métis history, see Chapter 11.

31

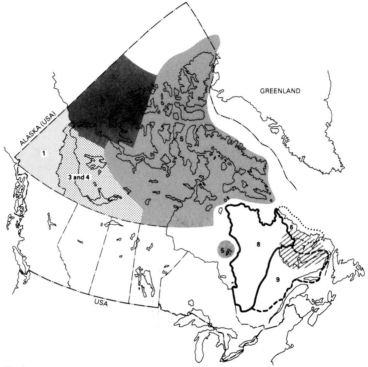

The future

4. *The areas of northern Canada as defined by aboriginal*
   peoples or modern agreements between them and the federal
   government.

1. Council for Yukon Indians' land claim
2. Inuvialuit territory
3. Denendeh (Dene) territory
4. Métis territory
5. Nunavut (Inuit) territory
6. Labrador Inuit Association claim area
7. Naskapi-Montagnais Innu Association claim area
8. James Bay and Northern Quebec Agreement area
9. Conseil Attikamek-Montagnais claim area

Overlaps and claims in western provinces are not shown.

source: Canadian Arctic Resources Committee, *Northern Perspectives* 13(5), 1985.

The hunters and trappers probably number between 70,000 and 100,000, of whom roughly 24,000 are Inuit, 17,200 Dene, 11,700 Cree, 470 Naskapi, 825 Innu and 3,200 Montagnais. However, no accurate population statistics exist. Persons classified by the Canadian government as Indian or Inuit are all named on administrators' lists. But among Dene and Innu, children of Indian mothers and white fathers often were not accorded official status as Native People. (Conversely, children of white mothers and Indian fathers were.) Although many of these children were brought up, and think of themselves as Indians, they do not figure as such in census data. Similarly, descendants of Europeans on the north Labrador coast who have merged culturally and economically with the Labrador Inuit are known as Settlers and are usually not recognized as a native group. Official data therefore have always understated actual numbers.

This short book is restricted to those regions and societies that find themselves in Arctic and Subarctic Canada, at the very edge of or beyond agricultural settlement and outside the economic and social influences of Pacific salmon. Their division from other cultures in central and northern Canada is artificial. Ojibwa, Tahltan, Carrier, Wet'suwet'en, Tlingit and many peoples of the north Pacific coast also depend on hunting and trapping, to say nothing of the multitude of societies in Alaska, the Soviet Union and Greenland. Much of the history, ethnography and politics of Subarctic and Arctic Canada applies more widely. The peoples of the Canadian north share compelling features, as well as some disturbing modern history, with others whose lives are also dependent on hunting, trapping, animals and northern lands. This book cannot speak of, but does speak for, many more peoples than it mentions.

Chapter 3

Cold

Mean Daily Temperature (°C)

	Jan	Feb	Mar	Apr	May	Jun	Jul	Aug	Sep	Oct	Nov	Dec
High Arctic (Arctic Bay, NWT)	−29.8	−31.1	−27.7	−19.8	−7.6	2.1	5.8	4.8	−1.6	−11.1	−21.1	−26.8
West Subarctic (Fort Smith, NWT)	−26.9	−22.6	−14.6	−3.2	7.1	13.1	16.1	14.3	7.7	0.5	−11.8	−21.4
East Subarctic (Schefferville, Quebec)	−22.7	−21.1	−14.8	−6.9	0.9	8.5	12.6	10.8	5.6	−0.9	−8.7	−18.1

During an average Arctic January, air temperature on a still day is between −24 and −36°C. In the Subarctic, the range is from −10 to −22°C. At latitude 70°N, along a line that cuts through northern Dene and Inuit territories, average temperature is above freezing for only three months of the year – June, July and August. Even at the southern edge of Inuit lands, Labrador and Hudson Bay coasts and islands are rimmed by sea ice for at least seven months each year. In the Subarctic boreal forests and interior tundra, the great maze of lakes and wetlands that shape the geography is frozen for eight or nine months each year. In summer, only the top few inches of Arctic soil ever thaw: below this, earth and moisture are seized in the rocklike continuum of permafrost.

Arctic and Subarctic societies must depend upon, and not simply exist in defiance of cold. Each of the cultures has its own ways of taking advantage of winter. Some of these are comparatively easy to see. All the fish in a frozen lake are vulnerable to a fisherman who knows where to cut an ice hole and lower a hook or use a leister, the three-pronged spear. Caribou moving south to escape High Arctic winters can be intercepted, killed and cached in such numbers as to allow winter-long supplies of

*

An igloo is easier to keep up than a house. I don't remember ever being cold or uncomfortable in one. When it got too old and you had to patch it up every day, you just went ahead and built a new one.

Celine Ningark
Pelly Bay

I went south twice:
Edmonton, Saskatchewan.
It's hot down there – I went in July –
too hot to go outside.

Guy Kringorn
Pelly Bay

*

frozen meat and fat. Seals that winter in the far north must have a breathing hole in the ice to reach the air where they are vulnerable to harpoons and guns. New ice, both on sea and lakes, provides excellent travelling conditions for a dog team: a hunter can cover large areas in pursuit of fishing places or seals' breathing holes, and can make kills with comparatively lightweight and elegantly simple technology. Snow in Subarctic forests means that moose, which move into known wintering grounds in sheltered valleys and areas of good willow browse, leave clear tracks. Spruce and ruffed grouse collect in groups, and are easily found gathered in tree roosts. Rabbits' tracks in snow make them easy to snare. So long as caribou, moose, seals, fish, overwintering birds and smaller mammals are plentiful, Arctic and Subarctic hunters can provide themselves with an excellent diet throughout – and thanks to – winter.

Hunters who use lie-in-wait strategies, like Inuit at breathing holes or hiding behind stone cairns, rely on caribou-skin clothing. In early autumn, when growing their new winter coats, caribou provide the most effective insulation. The density of new hair is remarkable, while each follicle is hollow: the caribou covers itself with a cushion of air. By skilful preparation of these hides and sewing seams with astonishingly tight stitching, northern hunters can insulate themselves against almost any weather. Dressed in two layers of caribou hide – the inner fur against the skin, the outer toward the air – a person can safely sit or even sleep in the open at −30°C. Thus dressed, anyone who walks in soft snow or up even a shallow incline will quickly overheat and need to remove the outer layer of clothing. Each northern group celebrates the importance of these caribou-hide suits with a profusion of local designs and ornamentation.

In the Subarctic boreal forest, where tracking animals on foot is a central hunting strategy, clothing is surprisingly light. Here, movement is relied upon to generate warmth; when not moving, hunting families quickly build large fires. For them, suppleness

and durability of skin clothing are of prime importance, and to this end they wear a single layer of caribou, fur against the skin, or prepare caribou, moose and deer hides from which the fur is removed. Cree are famous for their blankets and capes woven from rabbit skins.

Winter housing also takes advantage of the cold. The most famous example of this is the *igluviga*, the snow house. (*Iglu* is an Inuit word for interior or any form of dwelling.) Made from blocks of wind-packed, dry snow, an *igluviga* can be erected in as little as an hour. The snow, like the hair of caribou, traps air within its structure, and so means that the snow house has the excellent insulation offered only by still air. Inside, a seal oil lamp or a single-ring camp-stove provides enough warmth for people to sit comfortably in a single layer of clothing, or even stripped to the waist. Heat generated by the lamps or stove rises to the crown of the house, and causes trickles of melting snow to run down the domed sides. In cold weather, these freeze as they reach the lower, colder parts of the walls. Too much warmth outside and inside can cause chunks of slush to drop into the house. This result of insufficient cold is relieved by placing a low skin roof inside the snow house.

In fact, only a minority of the world's Arctic peoples ever made use of snow houses. Most Eskimoan peoples built *karmat*, stone, whalebone and sod huts at winter village sites. These are warm, however, only when blocks of snow are heaped around them. Even in the central and eastern Arctic, regions that made the snow house world-famous, many if not most families living on the land throughout the winter use *karmat* rather than *igluvigat*. In the Subarctic, Athapaskan and Algonquian groups build wood cabins or improvise wood and canvas or wood and hide shelters. In some cases, these are banked up by snow to provide insulation, though all rely on wood fires for heat.

Modern housing has brought prefabricated bungalows, electric cookers and oil-fired furnaces to all parts of the north. One

result has been overheated, humid houses, with consequent increases in infectious diseases. Most northern people, however, welcome the amenities of village life. But they continue to rely on cold. Meat is cached in rock pits, on roofs and in cold porches. Snow houses, cabins and bush camps are essential for the hunting and trapping that continue to provide food and identity to every northern family.

Europeans, with their agricultural heritage, react with fascinated horror to the idea of far northern cold. This fascination leads to some overstatement: children's books about the Eskimo and popular writings about the Arctic often insist that there is no summer, that land and people are gripped in a savage twelve months of snow and ice. Horror is aroused by, and expressed in, descriptions of the far north's lack of biological productivity. A region where only a handful of birds can survive winters, which even caribou desert in autumn, where vast lakes contain only one or two species of edible fish, and whose chilly seas support only a limited range of marine species – this would seem to be a region beyond the margins of civilization, a place where human beings do not belong and cannot flourish.

A maximum of fifty bird species nest in the Subarctic and only ten to twenty in the Arctic. Caribou and Musk Oxen are the only ungulates in the barrens. Two species of seal live under the winter ice, and one of these, the bearded seal, is rarely found by hunters. But fish in the lakes, notably arctic char and trout, grow to extraordinary sizes, and at times can be taken in large numbers. Similarly, caribou herds are huge, in some cases numbering hundreds of thousands. And the ringed seal is abundant in every part of the Arctic coastline. Low biological productivity means that animals grow at a slow rate, or must effect sophisticated migrations. It does not prevent them from being large or numerous. And from the hunters' point of view, numbers and weight of animals and fish, not variety of species, establish the richness of hunting territories.

43

The biology of the far north is in fact both richer and more dependent upon the cold than may at first appear. Massive areas of shallow lake and swampy muskeg, resting on permafrost, can never seep away. Also, in the dry cold evaporation is minimal. Expanses of shallow water provide habitats for insect life. Swarms of small flies are nourishment for many birds and fish. At the same time, freshwater shrimp and the larval stages of these flies provide food for ducks, geese and char. The open tundra, where cold summers ensure that trees remain at a bonsai level a few inches above the ground, is the perfect habitat for the lichens, grasses and sedges that support caribou. Despite the cold air and permafrost, some 200 species of plants grow on some of the Arctic islands, while about 600 are found in the tundra and Subarctic forest. Throughout the land, therefore, the sunlight of spring and summer ensures that insects and grasses are converted into the protein upon which hunters depend. But the basic habitat is the result of extreme cold.

The sea offers a second biological support system that is also a product of coldness. Each year millions of small seawater creatures, including plankton, krill, shrimp and fry, move into Arctic and High Arctic waters. They do so to take advantage of microorganisms that have been growing at the base of the sea ice. As ice breaks, moves and melts in spring and summer, this nourishment – food for the small northward migrants – is released into the water. These small creatures are the prey of larger organisms: several species of seal, whale and dolphin. This food chain provides sufficient nutrients to ensure that a large population of seals can survive all year round in the Arctic.

As soon as the land is free of snow, along exposed hillsides and ridges, plant life in the far north hastens to take advantage of the brief summer ahead. Everywhere flowers begin to bloom, grasses form delicate and beautiful seed-heads, and berry bushes bear fruit. On High Arctic islands, where snow does not leave the land until June and sea ice is firm until late July, plant life

has found successful niches among fractured rock and in muddy tussocks in the muskeg. Above the Arctic Circle, the sun does not set in summer; at 70°N, there is continual daylight from mid-May until late July. Into this brief but sunny growing season, vast numbers of birds return to nest each year. Just one of several murre (guillemot) cliffs on Bylot Island, for example, has no fewer than 250,000 breeding pairs. Those who have been raised to think of the north as an impossible environment see these flowers and breeding birds as vivid outposts of natural beauty, a sort of defiance of the cold impossibility by representatives of civilization.

For hunters of the north, however, warmth can bring some of the most dire problems. Water is more dangerous to the traveller and hunter than is ice. A tundra awash with lakes and marsh means that sledges have to be abandoned in favour of walking, often in extremely difficult conditions. In summer, water is less saline and seals less fat: they tend to sink when shot, while open water is made dangerous for kayaks and canoes by unpredictable summer storms. Boreal forest in summer is thick with the tangle of undergrowth, and scarcely any less marshy than the tundra to the north. These are the worst conditions for tracking and snaring. And summer, for both tundra and forest, means swarms of biting flies that, whenever there is no wind, can make life miserable. When the weather is warm and wet, skin and fur become far less effective clothing. Sealskin boots and jackets can be watertight, but all hides soak up moisture and lose their insulating properties. Modern waterproofs keep out the wet but not the cold. Each summer, Inuit who trek inland to hunt caribou face high risks and endure some of their greatest physical hardships. Among Dene, Cree, Naskapi and Innu, summer is a time for finding an open area or coastal site that is relatively free of insects, and where the difficulties of summer hunting can be exchanged for the advantages of social gathering and relative inactivity.

47

Spring camps in both the Arctic and Subarctic are happy and active places. Inuit, making use of canoes at the ice edge or on the newly open sea, can hunt new areas, find young seals basking on the ice, and make their way to the nesting sites of sea birds to collect eggs. Dene and Cree move to beaver ponds, where they can enjoy the excitement and contemplate the financial benefits of hunting beaver as they swim from their lodges. But these spring camps are short-lived. Once summer is in full swing, and flies begin to swarm, it is the visitor from the south, the European explorer or North American biologist, who thinks that this is the time to be in the north.

When lakes freeze, sea ice re-forms and firm snow creates good travelling conditions, hunters can once again begin to move about their territories with ease. Nowadays, excitement at the coming of another winter finds an echo in the throbbing of snowmobile engines and parties of hunters and travellers who once again can take advantage of living with and from the cold.

Chapter 4

Meat

Vitamin C Content in Meat Diet
(Minimum required to prevent scurvy
c. 10mg/day)

	Raw	Cooked
	Ascorbic acid (mg/100g)	
Seal meat	0.5–3	0.5–2.5
Seal liver	18–35	14–30
Whale skin (narwhal)	18	n.d.
Whale skin (beluga)	35	n.d.
Blubber (beluga)	5	n.d.
Animal meat (caribou, musk ox, polar bear)	0.8–1.8	0.5
Fish (cod, char)	0.5–1.8	n.d.
Cod roe	44	n.d.
Birds	1–2	0.3–1

Source: H. W. Rasmussen (1939), 'Vitamin C sources in Eskimo food', *Nature* 143: 943.

The hunting cultures of the far north are based on an almost pure meat and fat diet. Krill and small fish dependent on krill are too small to be caught and processed for human consumption. Seals convert them into larger packets of muscle and fat. Although Inuit do eat warble-fly larvae that grow in caribou, insects and pupae are not much use as human food. But fish grow large and fat on pupae and larvae; hunters can catch and eat char and lake trout. The human digestive system cannot unlock the nutrients in sedges, lichens or mosses. But the vast herds of caribou manufacture meat and fat, whose protein, vitamins and calories are easily absorbed by the human system. Moose and mule deer do the same to the growing tips of willows and other plants for hunters of the Subarctic. Both bears and people eat fish and berries, but people also eat bears (they even mix their fat with berries).

In Inuktitut, the language of the Inuit, the word for eating (*niri*) and meat (*niqi*) are strikingly similar. In fact, *niri* is a root used for food as well as the various forms of the verb to eat, while an expression that can best be translated as real food, *nirimarik*, refers to meat from wild animals. The words for fat, *uksuk* and *tunnuk*, distinguish between the fat of sea and land animals respectively. The vital importance of sea mammal fat in many Inuit diets (the large exception being the caribou-dependent peoples of the inland tundra) is revealed in the use of *uksuk* as a root for the word for petrol and stove oil, *uksualuk*, upon which modern hunting and cooking depend. The Dene make a similar connection in their ancient histories, saying that the white man's energy comes from wells that trap the fatty remains of ancient animals.

In northern meat-eating societies, animals are butchered, prepared and stored with great skill and enthusiasm. Understood and properly treated, meat is both nourishing and a basis of sophisticated, varied tastes.

When Inuit hunters kill a ringed seal, they often eat raw liver mixed with small pieces of fat, or fresh ribs, while the carcass is still warm. Once frozen, the texture and flavour of the meat changes; pieces sliced from the back and limbs are especially good. Intestine, fresh or wind-dried, is a delicacy. All parts of the seal are also boiled in carefully butchered sections, and eaten hot. Seal meat that has been stored in semi-subterranean rock caches is one of a range of *igunaaq*, the Inuit equivalent of cheese: meat, fat and skin of each species acquire a distinctive, strong flavour as they slowly decay in store. Appreciation of *igunaaq* is an important and sophisticated feature of Inuit taste, as is the careful choosing and combining of other parts, species and conditions of various animals, birds and fish.

Among the Dene of the Subarctic, freshly killed moose meat is barbecued in strips in front of open fires. Most of a kill, however, is taken to camps or villages where it is shared among house-

holds. Some is eaten fresh, and some – like meat hung in good butchers' shops – develops a richer taste and altered texture as a result of being kept longer in a porch or lightly smoked alongside open fires. The skills and joys of eating moose require an appreciation of these changes.

Among Subarctic hunters, however, the most important way of preparing meat is in the making of the famous dry meat – the lightest, most concentrated source of protein known to human cultures. This is done by women, who take large pieces of fresh meat and cut them into long, very thin strips. They lay these on frames set above smoky fires. Every few hours they turn the strips until they are completely dry and permeated with smoke. The dried strips are then piled in heaps, covered with a skin or tarpaulin and jumped on. This further compresses and flattens the meat into a most portable form. Spread with fat or lard, dry meat is eaten both as a complete meal in itself and as a delicious supplement to other meats.*

Northern hunters point out that they waste very little of an animal, leaving only lungs, genitals and other small amounts of entrail in the bush or on the ice. Everything else finds its way into their diet, or becomes raw material for clothing and artefacts. Brains are rubbed into hides as a skin softener and preservative. Spinal and leg tendons are used to make thread. Seal windpipes and intestines can serve as snow-house windows. Fish skins can be turned into strong and compact needle and fish-hook cases. Ptarmigan bladders make children's balloons. Fish eyes are a treat – rather like snacks for children. Boiled ducks' feet are fun to eat. The bones of a seal's flipper make all the pieces for an

---

* Inuit prepare a similar form of dry meat from caribou, seal and char. The dry air of the High Arctic makes it possible to achieve the same result without the use of a fire: strips can be laid out on rocks to dry in the wind and sun. In most Inuit dialects, *nikku* is the name for dried animal meat and *pisik* for dried fish. In Athapaskan languages the many words include *beg 'uné* (in Slavey) and *bog 'on* (in Dogrib).

elaborate Inuit game. A goose or ptarmigan wing is an excellent duster.

In all northern regions, plants, roots and berries supplement or flavour the meat diet. Inuit eat bearberries, cranberries, blueberries and huckleberries. Dene and Cree gather, dry and store blueberries, huckleberries, cranberries, raspberries and strawberries. The Cree in particular are famous among hunting peoples for their use of roots, bark and herbs as food and medicines. Inuit eat the flowers of long-stemmed arctic poppies and the leaves of some of the saxifrages and miniature rhododendron that crouch in the tundra. Arctic and Subarctic hunters will also eat the roots of wild parsnip and the root of a sedge that has a cluster of rice-like nodules. But the rich, nutritious and – when understood and appreciated – delicious staple is a mixture of meat and fat.

Much has been written by Western dieticians about the advantages of a mixed diet, in which a small amount of meat is balanced by comparatively large amounts of cereals and pulses, vegetables, fruit and milk products. In the course of the twentieth century, emphasis on plant foods in this balance has become strongly associated with health. Vegetarians, from strict Vegans to those that allow milk products, eggs and fish, have achieved a remarkable ascendancy within the ideology of nutrition, and meat has been made to carry the blame for high incidences of heart disease, cancer, diabetes and even aggression.

Indeed, a feature of the stereotype of the Inuit is an image of a savage gorging on raw meat and blubber. Alongside this deprecating, even disdainful stereotype is quasi-scientific incredulity. One of the questions most often asked about Arctic and Subarctic hunters is, how do they get their vitamin C? A more modern question would be, why are they not all dying of heart disease? Condemnation of the environment has its dietary counterpoint: to survive at all in such a place, you must reduce yourself to the level of a disagreeable and probably unhealthy carnivorous

animal. The widespread belief that a mixed or vegetarian diet is the only guarantee of good health provides a rationalization of the judgement passed by southern, agricultural cultures upon those of the north.

In fact, a diet of meat and fat provides everything human metabolism requires. Recent medical surveys show a low level of cholesterol and low incidence of diabetes among Inuit. Meat, raw or lightly cooked, contains sufficient vitamin C for human needs, while certain items of Arctic diet – notably whale skin and seal liver – contain vitamin C in very high concentrations. Early explorers and whalers who overwintered in the Arctic knew nothing about vitamin C or its relationship to scurvy, but found that as long as they could keep their crews supplied with fresh meat, especially when their bottles of lime juice had burst in the cold, they stayed healthy throughout the winter.

Between 1918 and 1928 Vilhjalmur Stefansson urged American public and scientific opinion to appreciate the nutritional advantages of a pure meat diet. He used his own findings among the Inuit of the western Arctic, dental data relating to all northern cultures (including the Norse), and ethnographic common sense in support of his view that, far from being dangerously incomplete and nutritionally retrogressive, after a few weeks of adjustment, an all meat and fat diet is ideal for human health.

In 1928, having failed to make much headway against mixed diet or vegetarian opinion, he and a colleague undertook a one-year controlled experiment; they ate only meat and fat and were monitored by a medical team at Bellevue Hospital, New York. Public and scientific reaction to this experiment, the results of the project, and Stefansson's many findings and arguments on the cultural, historical and nutritional importance of meat, are detailed in his book *Not By Bread Alone*. Briefly stated, these results give strong evidence in support of Stefansson's meat-eating thesis. More recently, the American anthropologist Marvin Harris has reviewed the idealization of meat and fat among

*

I would like to say a few words about this land.
The only food I like is meat.

Salluviniq
Resolute Boy

I thought, I want to be at home.
I was starving – for fat, craving for meat
of wild animals. All we got to eat was leaves.
There were many of us in hospital. The doctor practically
had to force feed me, I was starving to death ... The only
things that I could eat there were the two eggs and
bread. But those leaves! The other stuff was
just boiled leaves, horrible vegetables.
They seemed as if they came
from the bottom of the sea.

Bettsy Crowe
Sanikiluaq

God created the world for us to live on
and hunt on for our food. God gave to us the world
to do that, so that's how we live. Animals that are on the land
belong to the land, and were created by God
for people to eat, for the people to hunt
and have the animals for food.
That's the only way I see it.

Tom Uvloriak
Nain

*

almost all human societies, providing a more or less universal endorsement of the northern hunters' point of view.

Diet in the north has undergone many changes. Sugar and flour have become large elements in many Arctic peoples' carbohydrate-loaded food. The medical results of this change are beginning to be understood. Obesity, eyesight deficiency and otitis media, with its high incidence of hearing loss, are all associated with the move from pure meat to modern, low-cost eating habits. The dental problem is also evident. Northern hunters on a pure meat diet show no signs of tooth decay, while modern Inuit and Dene children have among the world's highest incidence of dental caries.

Today's northern peoples continue to affirm the importance of meat. Detailed studies of Cree, Dunne-za and Inuit hunting show that hunters provide between one and two pounds of meat per day for each person. The problem, then, is not that hunters have ceased to hunt, or that meat is no longer available to their communities. Rather, the non-meat components of the diet are the source of dietary ills.

Stefansson points out in his work on this subject that a person who eats only meat must balance the protein with about 40 per cent, by weight, of fat. Human beings, however, adjust the balance within hours of eating: surfeit of fat to protein results in almost immediate nausea, while excessive protein produces fat craving. Left to themselves, so long as both meat and fat are at hand, people will naturally find a balanced diet. In the case of carbohydrates and sugars, however, the human body quickly develops tolerances and addictions that mean diet is not balanced by the feelings and needs that eating itself should create.

Hunters are often described as humans who perch at the margins of possible existence, stalked by constant fear of starvation. But hunters have suffered far higher instances of malnutrition and diet-related death as a result of modern, mixed diets than

they ever experienced from dependence upon resources that they knew how to find, kill and eat – and which provided an excellent balance of all that the human body requires.

Starvation there has been. Some authorities say that in the late seventeenth and eighteenth centuries climatic change resulted in animal redistribution that in turn caused temporary hardship for northern hunting peoples. At least as early as the 1820s the Hudson's Bay Company encouraged Indians not to move to traditional hunting grounds in winter, but to trap regardless of the availability of food species. In some places this resulted in starvation. But hunting has got a bad name in part as a result of the decline in wildlife caused by European activities. The bowhead whale and beluga – upon which the largest concentrations of Inuit depended – were virtually exterminated by European and American whalers between 1800 and 1900. Whalers also slaughtered walrus, one of the best foods for human beings and sledge dogs, in such numbers as to deplete both western and eastern Arctic stocks by up to 80 per cent. Similarly, white settlers and hunters in the Subarctic – notably during the gold rushes of the late nineteenth century and the spread of agriculture and white trapping between 1900 and 1930 – have caused decline or redistribution of ungulates, upon which Dene and Cree depended. But not all animal populations have been depleted. Caribou and moose are abundant, and now spread beyond their former ranges. In general, however, northern hunters had a safer existence – with more meat at hand – before the white man slaughtered tens of thousands of northern animals.

Even with these many changes, the adaptability and skill of hunters have meant that they continue to rely on meat as a dietary staple. Compared with the adventurers and explorers who visited the far north in the eighteenth and nineteenth centuries, the Inuit, Dene and Cree were well fed and healthy. Their lives must have been far more secure than those of the mass of the European peasantry and urban poor. Yet whites regarded nor-

thern hunters as destitute and marginal. Similarly, modern opinion can all too quickly conclude that here are among the poorest
of the earth. These 'poor' people, however, have at their disposal
an almost unlimited supply of the food that human beings, in virtually all cultures and at all times, most value: they can eat as
much meat as they like.

Chapter 5

Animals

*

One lady never wants to get married,
so her father asks her to marry a dog and she does.
When she gets children, they are puppies, so she puts them
into the bottom of her boots and lets them
float away, out into the sea.
The ones she tells: 'You will be white
people, *kablunaat*, and you will make things,
big things, smart, intelligent.' The others she tells:
'You will be Indians, you will hunt with bow and arrow.'
And they disappear. That is why *kablunaat* have so much hair
and are coloured like dogs. We call ourselves Inuit,
human beings, not animals. But we call you
Inuit anyway when we see you
in distance.

Armand Tagurnaaq
Baker Lake

They camped at the place he dreamed about
and one of his sons killed the fat moose he was told
of in his dreams. His son came back from the hunt and
they went out to get the moose. The other family went
with them then... The son asked his father,
'Aba [Father], how did you come to
dream that I would get that
fat moose? You dreamed right.'

Jumbie
Prophet River

*

In the earliest times, before life forms had found their limits and the world its shape, no clear line separated humans from animals. Many Arctic and Subarctic stories tell of sexual relations between people and birds and mammals. These brought about upheavals from which the world as we now know it took its form.

The Tlicho of the Mackenzie Valley originate from a woman's affair with a dog; the literal translation of the name is dog's rib. An Inuit woman who takes a lake monster as her lover turns into a fox, and then into blackflies. A man who sleeps with the fox-woman becomes a hare. The story of the most powerful spirit of the sea, Sedna or Arnaqapsaluk, begins with a union between a woman and a dog and ends with the creation of the mammals most vital to Inuit life.

Sexual relations with animals belong to an era that precedes the world we know. But the bond between humans and animals has continued; from it many people receive spiritual strength and insight. A blind Inuit boy becomes a loon* and regains his sight. A Dunne-za becomes a swan and is able to rid the world of monsters. These transformations are the result of special power, and from them come new powers. Hunters' and trappers' understanding of their environment and the powers that they need to thrive in it are built on an association between themselves, the animals and the land, for which stories about connection and transformation constitute the underpinnings and necessary system of belief.

Hunters and trappers know about animals. Their knowledge is detailed and intimate. The details and intimacy are a personal science, a system of understanding that reveals and secures the peoples' absolute dependence on the land.

* Great northern diver.

71

Dependence means, on the one hand, that hunters must kill animals in order to live. On the other hand, should animals go away or evade the hunter, people will starve. Dependence entails vulnerability. The relationship between the hunter and the hunted, therefore, has a certain equality. Ultimately, no one can be superior to that upon which he depends. This truth is expressed in the theory of life that underlies hunters' ideas about and attitudes towards animals, and yields what materialistic Westerners consider to be a spiritual dimension to knowledge.

Humans have souls and spirit powers. Humans and animals are equals. It follows that animals must also have a place in the spirit world. It also follows that animals too must depend upon the hunt; they must agree to be killed. All northern hunters insist that if animals are not treated with respect, both when alive and dead, they will not allow themselves to be hunted.* The hunt is thus a form of contract between partners, in which it is not always clear who is the prey.

The contract is not simple. Animals have to be found in vast terrain or dense bush. Or they must be intercepted on a trail that herds elect to follow each year. Under these difficult circumstances, how can the hunters find the animals? How can they be sure that the animals will let themselves be killed? This is their problem of knowledge.

Athapaskan and Algonquian hunters make contact with their prey in dreams of encounters with animals. Men and women who show proper respect for animals can leave their bodies at night and move along dream trails in the bush. The dreamer meets a moose or deer. The hunter notices a distinctive mark that identifies that animal. In the following days, when conditions are auspicious, the hunter goes out into the bush, finds

* In some regions, notably among the peoples living west of the Rocky Mountains, salmon transformation and spirit power are central to social and economic life. In all regions fish are of great importance.

the trail of the dream, and follows it until he discovers and recognizes the animal of the dream. Just as the animal allowed itself to appear in the dream, so it now agrees to be killed. The hunter collects the prey, as it were in fulfilment of a contract that was agreed in dreams.

Hunting with dreams is possible only if the hunter has dream power. This comes from spirit quests as a young boy or girl, during which spirit helpers are encountered. At the same time, the young person is taught to follow all the rules that embody a respectful attitude towards animals and the land. The dream hunt thus ensures, again and again, that interdependence between hunter and hunted is recognized and is continually made possible by mutual respect.

According to Dene, Cree and Naskapi theories of knowledge, success and happiness depend on the careful maintenance of good relations between people and all parts of the environment. The prime animals of the hunt – the large ungulates that provide stocks of meat and fat with a single kill – occupy a central place in hunters' dreams and spiritual concerns. But spirit power can come from any animal, including the smallest and least economically important. There is no spiritual divide between animals or, indeed, between animate and inanimate parts of nature. Spirit power can come from moose, bear or rabbits; but it can come also from rainbows and herbs. Northern hunters weave virtually every part of the natural world into a pattern of life in which each element is dependent upon the other.

Inuit hunters also insist upon a spiritual understanding of their environment and the interdependency between humans and animals. The weather itself is spoken of as a person, Sila. Speaking of fine weather, they say *silaqijuq*, Sila is absent; the word for rain is *siladlutuq*, Sila is upset. Similarly, Inuit often say that animals live on the land with the same kinds of needs and feelings as humans. When they kill an animal, hunters must acknowledge and placate its spirit. Inuit explain that seals allow

themselves to be killed because, living in the sea, they thirst for fresh water. In many parts of the Arctic, hunters trickle melted snow or river water into a dead seal's mouth, to assuage this spirit thirst. The same offering is made to freshly killed whales.

Many Inuit say that animals that are not hunted will decline in number. People have an obligation, therefore, both to respect the animal that is willing to die and to hunt animals to ensure that their species will thrive. In this double approach to animals, many hunting peoples express and seek to resolve a tension between respecting and killing animals. For them, respect is a system of wildlife management that includes harvesting.

When Europeans came to the New World and discovered its abundance of valuable animals, they proceeded to slaughter with a greed that was fuelled by the demand for fine furs, oil, whalebone and ivory. Northern hunting peoples came to be implicated in these trades, and responded to incentives to increase their harvests. They acquired the means – rifles and steel traps in particular – to kill some species with relative ease. A seal hunter with a harpoon waiting at a breathing hole for the animal to come to him is just as efficient as a man with a rifle. But caribou and polar bear hunters, whose older methods of killing required the hunter to approach within striking distance of a few yards, can use rifles to deadly effect. And even where the hunting equipment itself made no real difference to the ability to kill, European forms of transportation meant that dozens of traps could be set and checked in a short time, while large numbers of carcasses could be moved quickly and easily to camps, cache and trader.

In the James Bay region in the late nineteenth and early twentieth centuries, intensity of trapping for the fur trade resulted in such severe decline in beaver populations that its disappearance from an extensive area seemed imminent. This was checked by an extreme conservation scheme agreed between trappers, Hudson's Bay Company officials and the provincial govern-

Whatever kind of food I wanted,
if I wanted caribou I'd go up in the mountains;
if I wanted coloured fox, I went up in the mountain;
in the Delta I get mink, muskrat; but I never make a big
trapper. I just get enough for my own use the coming year.
Next year the animals are going to be there anyway,
that's my bank. The same way all over
where I travelled.

Bertram Pokiak
Tuktoyaktuk

The white man is going to come
and flood the land. That's teaching Indians
how to flood land and build dams. But the Indians can teach
the white man about nature. We have lived with nature.
We were born with it, we have got to look after it, not
to destroy it. It's like our mother. To us it is like
putting something in the bank when we do
not kill all the beaver we could. We
leave the beaver to allow
them to multiply.

William Matoush
Mistassini

When they're trapping,
the Indian people have their own world.
It's a totally spiritual world you live
in when you're trapping.

Willie Awashish
Mistassini

ment: beaver regained their former abundance.

Throughout the Arctic and Subarctic, selling furs to southern markets is an integral part of what the people themselves regard as their tradition. Understanding the fluctuations of white fox populations, anticipating the seasonal movements of lynx and marten, recognizing the tracks of otter and mink, knowing the ways in which beaver can be taken at different times of the year, being able to skin and prepare delicate fine furs, and knowing how to bargain with white fur buyers – these and similar kinds of knowledge and skills allow hunters to be successful trappers. Since the recovery of the beaver population, there has been no other example in the Canadian north of Inuit or Indian hunters' and trappers' activities threatening the stocks of any animal species.

At times, Inuit, Dene and Innu have been blamed for decline in caribou herds. Inuit have been accused of overhunting polar bear. But in every case where the cause could be identified, it emerged either that the decline was part of the natural population cycle or a result of European or Canadian activity. Since hunters throughout the north have been engaged in the fur trade and have used rifles for several generations, there is very little reason for thinking that modern hunting techniques have overwhelmed the peoples' ways of limiting pressure upon wildlife. Replacement of dog teams by snowmobiles in most areas has reduced each hunting family's daily need for meat. The supply of furs to the fur trade has also decreased since the 1930s.

Since the early 1970s, Inuit hunters' harvest of polar bears has been limited by a quota system set up and enforced by the Canadian federal government. Each village is allotted a number of 'tags', each one of which is worth a bear. Once all the tags are used up, hunters who kill a bear risk criminal proceedings. A similar quota system has been attempted for narwhal, the unicorn-like dolphin that appears each spring in the north-east

High Arctic, and whose skin is a delicacy and ivory a valuable trade item.

Inuit reaction to these quota systems has been mixed. Many elders take the view that all animal management is a matter for their own judgement, and restraint, especially if applied by inexperienced or uncomprehending southerners, will damage rather than help the bear and narwhal populations. Animals depend on being hunted. Others will agree that species at risk must be protected by a reduction in hunting, but dislike such proposals coming from and being enforced by outsiders. Nonetheless, the polar bear quota system seems to have achieved some of its intended effects: bear populations in the central and eastern Arctic appear to be strong and growing.

Northern hunters and southern conservationists can agree that animals must be protected. Ideas about protection may vary, and sometimes oppose one another. They are deduced from different theories of knowledge. Newcomers' claims to understand animal population dynamics can appear as something between naïve presumption and imperialist arrogance.

Biologists, on the other hand, point out that questions of conservation have become international. Northern hunters' systems of belief, harvesting and management may take into account only one part of a species' cycle. For example, geese that are harvested by Cree and Inuit as they move towards their nesting grounds are also hunted by white sportsmen or damaged by loss of winter habitat along the Mississippi Valley. Some caribou populations migrate deep into the boreal forest, where they are subject to pressure from white settlers. For these reasons, environmentalists sometimes argue, northern hunters must participate in inter-regional and international accords about ways in which some species can be protected in the long term.

The two sides of the argument at least share a common belief in the importance of wildlife as part of the natural world and as an economic resource for the peoples of the north. One can

imagine northern hunters and white biologists sitting down together, agreeing about wildlife problems and discovering ways in which these can be ameliorated. And there is no reason, in principle, why international agreements should not assume that one, perhaps the most important, objective is to ensure that hunters and trappers continue to be able to harvest animals in ways and numbers that they regard as necessary.

A certain optimism might be possible, therefore, if it were not for another intrusive way in which southerners presume to know what is best for animals. This is the animal rights movement.

Since the middle of the nineteenth century, European humanitarianism has included a campaign against unnecessary cruelty to animals. The focus was on the treatment of domestic pets and farm animals: early animal rights advocates considered shooting grouse, partridges, pheasants or other wildfowl, and hunting foxes for sport as necessary and proper. The original distinction between pets and wild creatures has now tended to become blurred. A campaign against blood sports (the killing of animals for pleasure) moved the debate away from the question of pets and the farmyard. Even here, however, it was a question of putting our own house in order; hunters and trappers who lived by hunting and trapping, and who in any case existed in jurisdictions far removed from our own, were not a matter of concern. Then in the 1970s and 1980s new organizations with a broad and international approach began to lobby against all harvesting of whales and the killing of harp seals off the Newfoundland coast. This soon spread into a general campaign against sealing and trapping.

The effect of the modern animal rights campaign on northern hunting peoples has been dramatic and, by and large, uncontrollable. Brigitte Bardot and the large eyes of the baby harp seal made a powerful appeal to the sensibilities of the world. But for the most part the world knew little of the difference between harp seals and ringed seals, bowhead whales

and belugas. Sealskin prices tumbled and the International Whaling Commission was pressured to effect an international ban on all hunting of whale and dolphin species – though some special consideration was given to aboriginal subsistence hunters. Ringed sealskin prices fell from approximately $30 to as little as $2 or $3 each. The economic basis of hunting families and, in the eastern Arctic, whole communities collapsed. In the grip of moral righteousness, animal rights activists have been slow to recognize that their campaign had become a new example of southern, imperialist intrusion.

Northern hunting peoples had been pressed into the fur trade by an earlier intrusion. The resources and wisdom of European economists were brought to the far north to create trappers who would serve European purposes. With some difficulty, hunters adjusted their socio-economic systems, and developed – in a characteristically flexible manner – a modernized traditional life. The newcomers succeeded: northern hunting peoples are now dependent upon trading skins and other renewable resources to southern markets. The advantages of this new tradition, when compared with other modern possibilities, lie in the extent to which respect for animals, concern with the environment, and love of the land itself have ensured that even the peak of the fur trade did not result in the extermination of a single species. Caribou populations are as high as they have ever been. Ringed seal appear to be thriving throughout the north. The moose population has expanded, and has now spread for the first time into Subarctic areas between the Rocky Mountains and the Pacific coast. Beaver, even in the James Bay area, where they once appeared to be in danger, are abundant throughout the Subarctic. Lynx, marten, fox, mink and wolverine are distributed as widely as they ever were. The hunters of the north say that the best way to protect the animals and the land on which they depend is plain to see: leave it to them.

Chapter 6

Mobility

*

If you look at the land,
it all seems the same, but some parts
of it are rough, with rocks all around . . .
But even on rocky land, if there is moss, that is where
the caribou stay during warm seasons. That kind of
land we used to occupy. We did not stay right
on one spot, expecting the game would
always come back there . . .

Evalak
Hall Beach

We do not just stay
in one place. We, the Inuit move around,
and we do not go home to just one snow house. We, the Inuit,
are trying to survive. We, the Inuit, do not just stay
in one place, neither in summer
nor in winter.

Inukshuk
Baker Lake

*

Hunters are always ready to move. This is a matter of economics. It is also a cultural habit, an approach to life, a way of dealing with the psychological and spiritual as well as the material demands of existence. Flexibility and mobility are at the heart of living in the north.

Each northern culture has its seasonal round, its pattern of movement from camp to camp, hunting area to hunting area. Hunters follow changes in weather, snow or ice conditions and the movements of animals. As they follow this annual round, hunting families travel familiar routes and reoccupy sites that have been important to their people for generations. The seasonal round occupies grooves of cultural history, and draws upon archives of experience and knowledge. Hunting itself, however, must defy habit as well as follow it: no two seasons are identical, animal migrations are never wholly predictable. Hunters, following well-worn trails, must seize new opportunities, adjust the pace and direction of their movements to follow, intercept or find the animals upon which life depends. At each point along the seasonal round individuals must assess and process a mass of information. The habit and pattern of mobility set the scene; action within the scene keeps changing.

The Cree of northern Quebec move inland every autumn to spend the winter within the treeline. Small family units camp together, often several days' walk from their nearest neighbours. These hunting groups are scattered over large territories, where daily life is divided between two kinds of harvesting: pursuit of large ungulates – such as moose – that must be tracked across many miles of forest; and the taking of smaller animals – such as rabbits, grouse and trout – that can provide a more reliable if less nutritious source of food. This division between large game animals and smaller prey is of immense importance. For the most

part, big ungulates, as important for their fat as their protein, are tracked by men. Over a year, their kills may provide the necessary quantity of meat and fat. But the supply is uneven, with large amounts of meat followed by none. Total commitment to large prey would lead to starvation. In fact, the continuous food supply – small mammals, birds and fish – is harvested by women as well as men on days when they decide not to, or fail to track large species. The men's hunting is endowed with importance of every kind. In reality, however, women's harvesting – precisely because it is less risky – often yields the food upon which families really depend. At the same time, women ensure that men can afford to devote several days to hunting moose, deer or bear without endangering their families. Winter mobility reduces the risk, but without the safety net of small species, winter tracking would otherwise entail real dangers.

In the winter forest, people have the advantage of protection against Arctic wind, wood to make fires and access to beaver and fish under the ice. Deciding when to move and which area to go to next, hunters take into account past and present conditions and predict the likelihood of finding all that people need at a particular spot.

The people of Labrador and northern Quebec also move inland every autumn, to intercept southward-migrating caribou and then to spend the winter within reach of the caribou's wintering grounds. Here again, small groups move over a large territory and must make a multitude of small adjustments to their camps and hunting techniques to ensure a reliable supply of meat and fish. In similar manner, the Athapaskan groups of the western Subarctic and Arctic spread out into autumn, winter and spring hunting grounds in the boreal forest, in pursuit of moose, deer, fish and the various small animals upon which they can depend. Late summer and early autumn are also the seasons for drying or smoking trout and white fish. This means families set up camps at prime fishing spots for as long as runs or stocks

need to be harvested. Large quantities of fish are prepared for winter use. Once more, this means that people scatter over many parts of their territories.

Inuit patterns of movement work in reverse. In spring or early summer families disperse into small groups in wide-ranging camps. There they hunt for seals basking on the ice and at their breathing holes. Then families begin to move inland to fish at lakes and hunt caribou. This movement to inland hunting territories continues throughout the summer, and family groups reconverge with other groups at the beginning of winter, when they all return to the sea ice and the seal hunt.

One Canadian Inuit group, the so-called Caribou peoples of the Barren Grounds west of Hudson Bay, spend all year living inland. Their seasonal round is shaped by movements to different caribou migration routes and feeding areas. Abundance of lakes and relative proximity of the treeline mean that fishing and wood gathering have special importance. But the Caribou people have an annual round that has the same overall shape as the Inuit on the coast. They scatter from spring to autumn, and converge in larger groups each winter.

Hunters make thousands of critical decisions each year. The processing of this information leads into the domain of spirituality and metaphor, where accumulated knowledge, intuition and the subtlest of connections with the natural world can generate choices on a basis that is quicker and surer than a narrow rationality. In this way, the decisions of hunters are close to the certainties of artists. By denying a reduction to a limited set of variables, the fullness of both culture and consciousness come to bear on each day's activities. The mobile and flexible behaviour of hunters is inseparable from this state of consciousness, this form of decision-making. Actions cannot be planned long before they occur; too many of the important variables are constantly changing. There can be no long interval between a decision to act and the action itself. By the same token, there can be few

simple continuities and little formal organization: hunters must respond to an ever changing environment with quick alertness. Each individual or small group plans and alters plans with a spontaneity as swift as it is subtle. There is no room for committees, organizers or institutional formality.

Readiness to move in order to ensure successful hunting can hardly be exaggerated. In the case of some northern Athapaskan peoples, hunters track moose and families track the hunters. When a kill is made, the hunters stop to butcher and prepare meat; the families then catch up with them, and a camp is made close to the kill. Soon the hunters move again, tracking more moose. They rarely stay in one place for more than three or four days. Similarly, once the main caribou migrations have passed, hunters of the barrens shift camp whenever they find that animals are too far away to be reached easily. Inuit of the Arctic coastline spend the long spring, from April to July, moving from camp to camp, from lake ice fishing to seal hunting along the shoreline, from nesting sites of migratory birds to spearing char as they return to the sea. Sometimes these movements occur with extraordinary frequency. Hunters set up camp one day, and decide the next that they have chosen the wrong spot and move on.

This nearly continuous movement is easily misunderstood. To people who come from settled cultures, where holidays are booked six months in advance and moving house requires a pantechnicon, where permanent residence and attachment to parcels of land are held to create the very possibility of human wellbeing, moving from place to place appears as an enormous burden thrust upon hunters by their poverty and improvidence. Far removed from the monotony of the rush hour, the intricate pattern of their annual round seems random and their hunting economy tenuous and insecure. In this way, early American colonists and even judges who heard early Indian rights cases characterized northern hunters as no better than beasts of the

field, roaming helplessly from place to place. Anthropologists have slipped at times into a misrepresentation of hunting economics as a haphazard, insecure, catch-as-catch-can existence.

But northern hunters' movements are neither random nor onerous. They follow well-tried patterns over intimately known terrain and are accomplished with technology finely tuned over thousands of years. They are the sum of experience and a proven system of harvesting the resources of the far north. Home is the territory as a whole. The seasonal gathering place may be where most continuous time is spent each year, but the network of camps, trails and travel routes – the territory upon which the hunting culture and economy depend – is a sort of total home. Strikingly, many Dunne-za when speaking English will ask 'Where are you staying?', in contexts where Europeans and North Americans would ask 'Where do you live?' In Inuktitut, people ask '*Naninunaqarpit?*' (where do you have land?) or will speak of the *miut* group to which you might belong. In the Inuit system of hunting areas, each *miut* group has a set of seasonal camps which constitute a basis for the annual round. From the hunters' point of view, irrational economic behaviour consists of excessive attachment to one place or too rigid and rationalistic forms of decision-making.

This mobility is as important for trapping as it is for hunting. Long before Europeans brought steel gin traps and snare wire, all northern peoples made some use of small animals' furs. Clothing was ornamented and trimmed with fox, lynx and wolverine. Blankets were woven from rabbit pelts. Shamans kept mink and marten skins in medicine bundles. Hunters took small numbers of these fine fur species with stone traps, deadfalls and snares made of caribou or moose hide. Other small animals, like beaver and rabbit, played an important part in diet. But most were available widely and predictably, and would never have shaped an individual hunter's decisions or a hunting group's seasonal round. Recent economic dependence on trapping has

brought many adjustments to seasonal rounds. But the basic patterns have remained much the same. Winter dispersal among Cree, Naskapi, Innu and Dene often means a move to trapping cabins in areas where fine fur species can be found. Once there, however, groups move in order to hunt for the animals that provide meat and fat.

But no human population can survive if it remains fragmented in small isolated groups. The seasonal round of all northern hunting peoples includes convergence in relatively large villages. Inuit gathering places are on, or near, winter sea ice. Subarctic hunters gather either at the coast, or a large river or lake, or in areas of natural or burnt-over meadow.* Open ground provides good habitat for many species of berries, which attract bears, whose fat can be mixed with the berries or dried meat that is also prepared at, or carried to, these summer camps. A village on the coast or lake shore and a camp in meadowland are relatively free of the Arctic's summer curse: here people can escape from hordes of biting insects.

The gathering place provides opportunities for exchange. Surplus produce can be shared. Liaisons and marriages can be arranged. And knowledge about animals and land can be pooled. Songs and dances, as well as stories and telling group histories, ensure the perpetuation and spread of knowledge. Bridges are built from the present to the past and between the natural and spiritual domains. Both kinds of gathering – in summer among the Dene, Cree and Innu, and in winter among the Inuit – occur at a season of comparative leisure. People have the time and opportunity to renew and revitalize their society.

* Many Subarctic peoples set fires, especially in spring, to burn out accumulated debris in the forest as well as to stimulate the growth of berry bushes and browse for ungulates. Burning also ensured that meadows stayed open. In this way, the seemingly natural openness of woods and alternation of forest and meadowland is part of the Indian peoples' shaping of the environment. Ironically, immigrant farmers established themselves on such open grounds, delighting in their 'natural' bounty.

*

We would net seals at Saglek
and hunt for them there and at Nachvak.
While at Hebron, we fished for trout or cod right on up to
Napatok. We would go caribou hunting farther
north or go south toward Nain. We would use most of the
lakes as routes for travelling. People from George
River and Hebron would meet in the
country when they were hunting.

Tom Okkuaksiak
Nain

Whenever a man hunts,
he does not hunt only for himself, so he has to be
assisted by the land where he is hunting. The game never moved
around in only one area. In some years the people occupy
some parts of the land, and at other times they occupy
another part of the land. The people from the
north used their land before, so they
know how to use it now.

Evalak
Hall Beach

*

Counterpart to their mobility is the hunters' rejection of materialism and their use of hunting technologies that are light, transportable and adaptable. The easiest place in which to carry technology is the mind. The hunter who can make a snare or deadfall out of materials he knows will be found at the hunting location need carry no more than a knife or axe. The harpoon with which Inuit hunt seals on the sea ice weighs only a couple of pounds. A bow and arrow weighs no more. Even a rifle can be slung over the shoulder. Equipped with these few pieces of hunting technology – plus a snow knife for making snow houses, needles and thread, three or four caribou hides as bedclothes and a cooking pot – an Inuit hunting family has enough to live more or less indefinitely. Subarctic hunters, especially those who travel by snowshoe rather than dog team, can rely on even less. Expertise with fires means clothing and shelter can be lightweight. This minimum of equipment, the absence of encumbering bulk, requires a confidence that each move on the hunting round will meet with success. Northern hunters do rely upon the storage of food, especially *igunaaq* or cached animals in the Arctic and smoked fish and dry meat in the Subarctic. They also eat as much as they can at one place, and thus carry excess within their own bodies. But readiness and ability to move is the key to living in the north. In this kind of society the highest possible degree of mobility represents a maximizing of economic efficiency.

The result is a form of economy that is deeply unfamiliar, and often very disturbing, to a society in which accumulation and surplus are accepted as the measures of social and economic success. For Europeans and North Americans, possessions represent security and prosperity. For hunters of the far north, accumulation of goods, including a large stock of foodstuffs, represents economic inefficiency, even incompetence. The two sets of criteria for judging economic wellbeing are opposite. Much of the dismay and anger traders, missionaries and other white agents of 'civilization' have felt towards unresponsive

101

native peoples stems from this fundamental economic opposition. The would-be benefactor gives his new native friends a heap of Western material goods. The delighted beneficiary expresses much thanks, explores the new goods, plays with them as if they were toys and then – when moving on to another place – leaves most of them behind on the ground. The trader urges the people to trap more furs, and offers higher prices as an incentive to trappers to increase the volume of trade. The trappers take fewer furs: higher prices mean that they can satisfy new needs (for flour, sugar, tobacco, tea and ammunition) with less trapping. Profound misunderstandings arise when representatives of settled, acquisitive cultures seek to help or to change mobile, hunting cultures.

Northern peoples' commitment to mobility, however, must not be seen simply as a matter of economics. It goes to the very foundations of life, receiving expression in the beliefs and metaphors by which life itself is defined. In the Inuit account of the creation of sea mammals, a man discovers that his daughter, Sedna or Arnaqapsaluk, has had sexual relations with a dog. The daughter is exiled to an island. She seeks to escape. In so doing, she tries to clamber aboard a boat that her father is rowing. Enraged, the man cuts her fingers as she reaches over the boat's edge: the joints fall into the sea, turning into seals, walruses and whales. Sedna herself sinks to the bottom, where she becomes the spirit presence who presides over the movements of all these animals that come from her own hands. On the surface of the water, the man must roam around to find the mammals at such times and places as the woman beneath will arrange for them to surface. Sensitive to any possible slight or disrespect, beneath the sea Sedna requires that the Inuit do not bring her creatures into contact with the animals of the land. Not only must the hunters move to find the surfacing sea mammals, they must keep a great distance between the two basic components of their lives, the animals of the sea and those of the interior.

*

Home is when I'm in the bush.

Charlie Bosum
Mistassini

We are not like the white people who go wandering
around looking for work. They are not like us ... who
have a home in one place. They, the white people, move
from one town to another, from one country to another,
searching for jobs to make money.

Agnes Edgi
Fort Good Hope

*

The mammals were created on a journey; they are harvested by a succession of journeys. Should Sedna be made unhappy by the hunters' failure to live in the right way, she becomes depressed. In her depression, she is unwilling to comb her hair. Her hair becomes matted; the sea mammals become entangled within her tresses. They do not find their way to the surface. The Inuit begin to starve. When hunters fail, therefore, one of them must make a journey to visit the woman under the sea, and ask her why she is unhappy, what rule has been broken. Thus the spirit journeys of a shaman are necessary to ensure that the mundane journeys of the hunters can continue to be successful.

Among the Dunne-za, a story that explains how the hunted and the hunter have changed places over time provides a symbolic version of how individuals must gain and use their powers. Here again, the culminating achievement is mobility.

A young boy lives with his father and stepmother. The stepmother takes rabbits shot by the boy and places them between her legs where, in their death agonies, they scratch the tops of her thighs. When the boy's father notices these marks, and asks how they have happened, the stepmother claims that it has been done to her by the boy. The enraged father takes his son to an island and maroons him there, to starve to death. On the island, the frightened boy cries himself to sleep. In his sleep he has a vision: he finds a way of attracting migratory ducks and geese, and is able to kill them and dry their meat. This dreamed knowledge makes it possible for him to live for a year. When the boy's father returns to the island to see in what manner his son has died, the boy escapes in his father's canoe, marooning his father in his place. The boy then returns to his stepmother and shoots burning arrows at her. When she runs into the water, the heat of the arrows' fires boils her down to bones.

All this takes place at a time when giant animals hunt people for food. The boy's mission is now revealed. He is given the name Swan. He becomes Swan, the white bird that appears with

strange beauty every year in the far north. Swan travels the paths of the sun, transforming monstrous animals into the creatures that humans can hunt and live from.

Hunters of the Subarctic grow to knowledge, adulthood and power with the help of dreams. This growth takes them on many journeys. In the course of a full life, they will travel the trails of the sun, under the mysterious inspiration of the magical swan.

In mobile, flexible hunting cultures, the guiding principle of human behaviour is egalitarian individualism. Each person must choose for her- or himself the trail to follow, the manner in which to lead daily life. No one seeks to enforce upon others a course of action or a pattern of choices. Children must grow at their own speed: good behaviour is not a result of authoritarianism. If one adult is unhappy about another's behaviour, the wise way to express the unhappiness is by moving away: to confront those one disapproves of is foolish and self-defeating. You ask for, and expect to receive, what you need. Sharing is not so much a social obligation as an acceptance of the right of others to have what they say they want. Each person is an authority on his own needs: the distinction between wants and needs, so important to Western cultures, is strongly at odds with northern hunting and trapping peoples' ideas and ideals.

Hunters' and trappers' mobility, which is at once economic, psychological and spiritual, has helped shape relations with white agents and agencies that have sought to alter northern peoples' way of life and claimed their land. Evasion is among the wisest reactions to difficulty. In so far as has been possible, therefore, hunters have taken advantage of new goods, ideas and economic activities while at the same time keeping their distance from the social and political forces at work. Groups move away, deeper into their hunting territories. Individuals retreat behind their own faces, hiding themselves from the white man – who sees only smiles or a sullen silence.

This means that newcomers in the north have not often encountered resistance to their presence or purposes. Only since the 1960s – partly as a result of limitations placed on the very possibility of their continuing mobility – have northern hunters and trappers begun to negotiate a relationship between the cultures. The European domination of the north and its people, therefore, is paradoxical: its achievements, from the hunters' point of view, have never gone as far or as deep as was supposed. Mobile, flexible, adaptable in holding to their own ways of behaving and thinking, the Inuit, Dene, Cree, Naskapi and Innu have succeeded in remaining true to themselves. They have absorbed much of what we would call white culture; but white culture has not absorbed them. They speak their own languages, raise their children according to their own principles, and live in a world that receives its deepest meanings from beliefs and metaphors that are their own.

Tepee with altar, Fort Simpson, *Government of the Northwest Territories, Tessa Macintosh, 1984.*

Inserting the final blocks to complete a snow house, eastern Arctic.
n.p., n.d., Government of the Northwest Territories.

Dene camp with fish drying, Mackenzie Valley, Northwest
Territories. *René Fumoleau, c 1980.*

Polar bear, Ellesmere Island. *Dan Orienti, 1983.*

Sleeping platform, Inuit camp, near Igloolik. *Bryan and Cherry Alexander, 1987.*

Easter races on snowmobiles, George River, Quebec. *John MacDonald, c 1972.*

Devon Island. *Dan Orienti, 1982.*

Walrus, Ellesmere Island. *Dan Orienti, 1983.*

Camp near Igloolik. *Bryan and Cherry Alexander, 1987.*

Elijah Nutarak skinning a polar bear, Ellesmere Island. *Dan Orienti, 1982.*

Corrine Shae preparing dry meat, Sansault Rapids, Mackenzie River, Northwest Territories. *Anne Cubitt, 1981.*

Hunter skinning a caribou, near Igloolik. *Bryan and Cherry Alexander, 1987.*

Dene preparing whitefish, summer camp, MacKenzie Valley, Northwest Territories, *n.p. c 1968, Government of the Northwest Territories.*

Walrus hunters, near Devon Island. *Dan Orienti, 1981.*

Netsilingmiut tends seal-oil lamp, inside a snow house, Pelly Bay, Northwest Territories. *G. M. Rousselière, c 1960.*

Dunne-za drummers, Halfway River Reserve, northeast British Columbia.
Anne Cubitt, 1981.

Wilbert Kochon holding wolf pelts, Colville Lake, Northwest Territories.
René Fumoleau, c 1980.

Chapter 7

Authority

*

Although our leaders
are very important to us: they
are meant to guide us and not to have power over
us ... For example, at one meeting one Dene asked,
'You, the leaders, where are you going to lead us?' And
one leader answered, 'We won't lead you anywhere ... A
Dene leader doesn't lead anybody anywhere. You
go where you want to go.'

Denendeh, A Dene Celebration

We don't grow up with a lot of rules.
Our parents don't get mad when we make a mistake;
they just help us and teach us.

Joanna Kiguktak
Grise Fiord

Our way is to try and give freedom to a person as
he knows what he wants.

George Barnaby
Fort Good Hope

*

In the language of the north-western Cree, the word used to mean boss or chief is *ugimau*. This, the only term that denotes institutional authority, is pejorative. The word for the person elected as chief under the modern political organization established by the Canadian Department of Indian Affairs is *ugimaxan*, literally, pretend or fake boss. This is a double pejorative.

In northern Athapaskan languages, there is no one term that is used for chief. In parts of Alaska, there is a word for leader, *dayan*, that seems to have its origins in some other, probably Siberian language. In several dialects, there is a composite expression meaning real person, and this is used to refer to chiefs. Among the Dunne-za of northern British Columbia, the word for chief is *mechee*, while the Indian agent is known as the *dunne-za mechee*, the people boss. In everyday usage *mechee* denotes parent or oldest relative.

Among the Inuit of the Baffin region in the eastern Arctic, the word most often used to mean authority is *angajurqaa*. The root of this appears to be *angajuk*, meaning older male sibling. There are similar words, however, that refer to other, older relatives (for example, *angak*, uncle). In everyday life, *angajurqaa* is used to refer to one's parents. It is also the name given to the Hudson's Bay Company manager or fur trader. In the central Canadian Arctic, the word *isumataq* is used for respected elder. This is based on *isuma*, thought or intelligence. Neither of these terms, *angajurqaa* or *isumataq*, can be directly translated as authority in European or North American terms. *Angajurqaa* is often used to imply undue bossiness. (A person teasingly asks of another: '*Angajurqaaraluuvutinnai?*' – You're a real chief, are you?) The need to find a way of explaining the position of prime minister often results in the construction of the composite word *angajurqaamarialuk*, extreme or thoroughgoing boss. In fact, Inuit,

despite their language's great facility for generating its own words for modern phenomena, tend to use English titles when it comes to the institutions of national and international authority.

As is the case in all societies, there are men and women among northern hunting peoples with extraordinary expertise. Some people have established connections with the supernatural world that allow them to explain natural phenomena, predict parts of the future, and cure many ills. Among Athapaskan and Algonquian peoples, some of these men and women dream their way along the trails of time, as well as to places above the earth from where they can see much that otherwise remains concealed. These are the shamans.

Shamans of the north receive their powers in vision quests, often as very young men and women, during which they discover what parts of the natural and supernatural world are going to be helpful to them. Sometimes these helpers are represented by amulets or medicine bundles that shamans always carry with them or place between their heads and the bush at night. Everyone in the community knows who the shamans are, and consults them if they need help, especially in cases of unsuccessful hunting and illness. Even the most powerful dreamers and medicine-makers, however, have no right to impose their knowledge or opinions upon others. They have powers, but not power. They have expertise, but not authority.

On rare but dramatic occasions, northern shamans have had visions with implications for an entire community. Dene dreamers have travelled to the sky and there been told of imminent danger, as in the example of the coming of whites, and have then campaigned for change in every household in their area. Inuit shamans have become convinced that they must move to a new territory, and have led a group of followers on migrations. A striking example of this occurred in north Baffin Island in the nineteenth century, when a group of Iglulingmiut travelled to a land a shaman had seen in a vision, and thus found its way to

north-west Greenland. Even this leadership is based on expertise. People follow the shaman in so far as they believe in him. He
does not have any means of enforcing his wishes other than the
respect or fear that his actual reputation arouses. Shamans
whom individuals reject cannot make an appeal to some other,
broader authority. The knowledge to which they lay claim is
often of vital importance to their fellows and would not be dismissed lightly. But their influence is individual; they are not an
institution.

Some men among the Dene are excellent trackers of moose.
One hunter might account for 60 per cent of all the animals killed
by a group of families in a year. Perhaps this is a result of his
powers as a dreamer, of the contract between hunter and animal
in which the animal agrees to be hunted, and according to which
the hunter must not betray the bargain by speaking of the dream
before the hunt takes place. This means that the hunter cannot
use his dream knowledge to guide the hunting of others. Perhaps
the exceptionally successful hunter can read the natural signs –
tracks, nibbled twigs, droppings, wind, topography – with
abnormal accuracy, and has reliable intuitions about the movements and habits of his prey. But this is not knowledge that he
could or would be expected to reduce to a set of instructions to
others. If the remarkable hunter of moose provides leadership or
constitutes an authority, it is because other hunters watch his decisions carefully, and fall in line behind him when a group makes
its way in single file along a trail through the bush. Each individual chooses his position; no one arranges others according to
hunting rank. If even the most effective hunter of all presumed to
give orders to companions, he would be said to be acting im-
properly. He is an expert, not an authority.

So how does a hunt take place? A group of men and women,
sitting at a campfire or in a cabin, talk about the land, animals
and the weather. A hunter with a reputation for great success as
a tracker of moose says that he thinks he will go to a particular

117

When an Inuk wants to hunt, he hunts;
he does not have to be told by other people.

Louis Alianakuluk
Igloolik

If I got some meat and somebody needs it, they come and
get a piece, and if I need some, I can go and get it.
Nobody gets left out.

James Ruben
Paulatuk

hillside the following day. Others say they might come with him, or propose the advantages of some other moose area. The next day comes. Nobody hunts. Something has changed: the wind perhaps, or a factor that can only be expressed as mood. Early the following morning, one of the best hunters says that he is about to leave to look for moose. He gathers up his gear, and sets off. As he leaves, others join him. A group makes its way to a place where they expect to find moose tracks – a natural salt lick, perhaps, or a known animal trail. They explore the ground. Each hunter looks by himself, but the findings are shouted out loud. After a while, the hunter with the strongest reputation chooses a direction in which to walk. The others, acknowledging his powers, have waited for this moment. They watch where he goes, and then, one by one, respond by choosing a direction of their own. No one organizes the overall collectivity of the hunt. But no one moves without reference to an understanding of what others are doing. There is no explicit system, but the overall effect is systematic. No one tells anyone else what to do, yet there is a tension between the hunters, a watchful waiting upon decisions by others. Should someone of lesser skills rush off on his own, ahead of everyone else, there will be no complaint. The more competent hunters will simply choose a direction in the light of what the impetuous novice may have done. The rarity of such an event is not a function of concealed authoritarianism. The imperative at work here springs from a communal wish for success and confidence it will be shared. Whoever makes the kill, everyone can help themselves to meat.

In these societies of equal individuals, community is based on membership of families. Membership of families, however, has a surprising double quality: on the one hand, everyone has powerful loyalties towards close kin; but, on the other hand, everyone in large bands or cultural groups insists that they are related to everyone else. Family connections establish strong obligations.

Blood and marriage ties underpin interdependence and co-operation. A basic security and equality are thus guaranteed.

Family membership also means that some individuals have extraordinary social standing. We have already seen that the words *angajurqaa* and *mechee*, while being used to mean boss or chief, also refer to parents or elders. This combination of meanings suggests the esteem that northern hunting peoples accord to the old. They say that to live is not easy, and to become old means you have known how to overcome many difficulties. Age is a measure of knowledge, a barometer of wisdom. Knowledge and wisdom command respect. In so far as is possible or practical, the young do what they perceive the old wish them to do. Elders' wishes and needs are anticipated and satisfied. This respect and anticipation of needs, however, means that the old do not need to exercise any outward authority. They offer advice; their advice is sought. More often, they do not advise so much as express a personal preference, which others will try to accommodate. But if the wish or advice does not accord with the judgement of an individual, that individual feels free to ignore even his most respected elder.

The oldest or most respected member of the largest or most successful family can appear to be a community leader. Even so prominent an individual, however, does not have a right to speak for others – unless the others have all agreed that this be done. Agreement requires a clear and public statement by each individual. In Inuktitut, the word *mali* means both to join a hunting party and to agree.

There is no institution of authority, no organization of power. These are cultures that refuse hierarchy, have not found any need for a language of intergroup or interpersonal authority, in which the expertise of dreamers and healers is deeply respected (and, at times, feared), but where not even the shaman is other than an important expert, a specialist with valuable but not controlling skills. In these societies, no individual can speak on

121

behalf of other individuals, neither parents for their children nor an elder for his family. No individual makes or enforces law. No group of individuals constitutes an assembly or equivalent to government. The individualism of the culture is a barrier against any form of organized domination; the egalitarianism a barricade against competitive individualism.

The men and women whose minds and lives have been shaped by hunting cultures know that in order to learn one must listen. They regard asking questions as, for the most part, intrusive, unnecessary and counterproductive. To make decisions about hunting, fishing, trapping and vital seasonal movements, individuals require immense amounts of information. Some of this is basic, factual and simple: you can find out where animals are, the condition of the terrain and opinions about weather, for example, by listening to other hunters describe their hunts. Some of the information is coded in the metaphor of dreams and shamanism: you can learn this by listening to the accounts of ancient history, stories, songs and dances told or performed by those who know best. Some of the information comes through one's own direct sense of the wind, the trees, the sea and the sky. Some is born in one's dreams. To receive and process the quantity and range of information necessary is, in theory, an immense, almost impossible task. Yet this is the information on the basis of which decisions must be made that can involve life and death risks.

There is a connection between the personal or intuitive processing of information and egalitarian individualism. Each person must decide for him- or herself. There is no authority, no institution upon which to rely. Success in this kind of system, for the individual and for communities as a whole, relies on a set of harmonies: between one another, between oneself and the natural world, and between oneself and the spiritual forces that can bring either success or disaster. These harmonies all entail an openness, a preparedness to listen and respond, a peaceable

*

When anyone comes asking for something,
I always give it, if I have it.
It doesn't matter if they can't repay you.
Ever since I can remember, my mother always used to
tell me that, even if I did not have very much, as long as
I had a bit to share, and saw someone without anything to eat,
she would like me to share with them. That was
how I was brought up. She would tell me that,
no matter how little I had, if I saw another
without food, I was to share mine.

Naeme Tuglavina
Nain

Respect for the old people
is another law, since all the laws
come from the teaching by our elders, from
stories that give us pride in our culture, from training
since we are young; we learn what is expected of us.
Without this learning from the elders our
culture will be destroyed.

George Barnaby
Fort Good Hope

*

engagement with one's own destiny. Interrupting a person who is speaking, looking for an authority to avoid personal responsibility, seeking to establish oneself as a dominant individual, failing to share openly and according to others' assessments of their own needs – in the world and ideology of northern hunters, these are all disruptive, self-defeating and wrong.

But even in an egalitarian and unauthoritarian social system there is bound to be a problem of deviance. In the absence of formal institutions, and in an interpersonal atmosphere in which individuals refuse to impose upon one another, how can deviance be prevented and dealt with?

Part of the answer to this question lies with hunters' mobility. Individuals or groups that cause trouble are avoided. This means that they will find themselves alone in a world where survival depends on a network of interdependence. The threat hanging over the head of all trouble-makers, therefore, is that their friends and relations will move away from them. In fact, northern hunting peoples are tolerant and generous to their fellows. A man who refuses to work, for example, will be fed: the sharing of meat is unconditional. But persons whose refusal to work begins to constitute a liability, and so jeopardizes others' success, are left to their own devices. In this way, the hunters' preparedness to shift camp establishes a strong deterrent as well as an actual, if indirect, reprisal. By this mechanism, deviance is rendered uncommon and, at the same time, can easily be dealt with.

People may refuse to be left behind. A trouble-maker might follow others, imposing his presence on them despite the strongest signs that he is unwelcome. And there is a limit to hunters' ability to move on. This, a real and dangerous deviance, appears to be very rare in northern cultures. It amounts to madness. But it is not unknown, and has been met with a simple remedy. Incorrigible deviance that menaced others in a

dangerous and direct way was dealt with by execution. Individuals whose behaviour amounted to madness that would not respond to shamanistic cures, patient tolerance or avoidance were killed.

As we shall see later, the arrival of white police and the establishment of Canadian law in the far north has meant that the peoples' ways of treating extreme deviants have been replaced or suppressed. Encounters with newcomers, however, have included executions according to Inuit law. In 1913 two Copper Inuit hunters killed two priests who were forcing them at gunpoint to make a journey they regarded as dangerous. In 1926, a hunter in north Baffin killed a white free trader who pursued Inuit families, demanding that they sell him their fox skins and threatening to shoot their dogs if they would not co-operate. In both these instances, the Inuit who killed white deviants were following their own law. In the case of the trader, the Inuit involved carefully carried his body, furs and papers to a white police outpost to ensure that the trader's relatives would not think that the Inuit had stolen their possessions. Both these killings resulted in dramatic trials, as a result of which the Inuit were given prison terms: the trader's killers got ten years and the priests' executioners were sentenced to life. Canadian law was made to prevail, though in the latter case reprieves after two years reflected an appreciation by the courts that the Inuit had done what they believed to be right. They were dealing with deviance in their own way.

The missionary and trader killings took place in parts of the far north where indigenous customs had remained isolated from white newcomers into the twentieth century. In other parts of the Arctic and Subarctic the absence of formal institutions of authority and leadership presented problems to the very earliest colonists. When colonial administrators began to oversee settler–native relations, they looked for spokesmen with whom to negotiate agreements. Their initial dealings were with the Iro-

quoian peoples of the eastern woodlands of what is now upper New York state, New England and south-east Canada. The Iroquois, with their maize fields and settled populations, are not egalitarian individualists. Indeed, their institutions of government and leadership are not unlike those of European nations. It is no coincidence that Marx and Engels saw a model of ideal democracy, an improved classical city state, in the accounts they read of the Iroquois system. This meant that colonial administrations could find chiefs among the Iroquois with whom to work out general accords. Hudson's Bay Company employees were able to adopt these dealings with chiefs and authorities in their relations with hunters and trappers in eastern Canada. As fur traders moved west, they took this model of dealings with them. They extended the fur trade, looking for and expecting to depend upon chiefs.

Under pressure from the demands of these white newcomers, and anxious to be able to take advantage of the guns and other useful goods they offered to trade, each Indian group tried to some extent to live up to what they thought traders expected. When it came to the issue of chiefs in the traders' dealings with the Athapaskan, Algonquian and Inuit, the potential for misunderstanding was great.

White fur traders needed someone who would understand them, represent the people and convey such decisions and instructions as Hudson's Bay Company officials chose to put in place. A go-between who spoke some of the newcomers' language could also be useful to the people themselves. Here was another kind of expertise. The northern hunters thus agreed, without any procedure of agreement, upon an expert; the traders, on the other hand, were certain that a chief had been chosen.

As the fur trade succeeded in creating new and growing needs among hunters for goods whose supply was monopolized by whites, elements of aboriginal territoriality and harvesting were

inevitably intensified. Family hunting areas in some regions appear to have been guarded with a new concern: harvesting by other groups might mean a loss of important buying power. This gave rise to new demands on elders' authority.

In the early days of the fur trade, therefore, family heads – especially among the western Dene and the James Bay Cree – sometimes represented their people on the basis of the specific individual consent that could go along with extended family membership. But pressures of fur trade negotiations and fur traders' inevitable ignorance of the subtlety of this kind of family representation meant that such elders were often pressed into a form of leadership that went far beyond its proper consensual base. Tragically, some important elders thus came to be used, and regarded by their own people, as messenger boys.

When the Canadian government sought to establish political institutions that would be compatible with those of the nation's mainstream, they also needed chiefs. Prior to 1940, Indian Agents assumed the power to select a man or woman and decree that he or she be chief. Subsequently, at a point when Indian Agents or their regional superiors had concluded that a people was 'ready', electoral procedures were established and chiefs chosen by popular vote. Now all chiefs and representatives are elected by the people of their community.

In the 1970s, some remarkable attempts were made to base new political processes on the family and egalitarian individualism. In the western Subarctic, Dene leaders set up decision-making bodies that relied on the consent of everyone in all communities. In doing this, they sought to ensure that Dene ways of making decisions and organizing social life be at the heart of a new politics. In areas where and times when this effort has not been made, even the peoples' own elected 'leaders' and 'chiefs' have found themselves at odds with the feelings and concerns of their people.

The results of the whites' need for institutions of authority have varied from extreme confusion, in cases where the supposed chief in fact had no real standing in the society, to quite effective compromise, where families and communities have ensured that elders and their own experts have a major say either in the choice of these new leaders or in the way in which they carry out their new (and sometimes very important) duties.

Systems of authority based on egalitarianism and forms of ownership based on sharing are so different from the hierarchical and competitive systems of Euro-Canadian culture that they tend to be invisible to newcomers. We cannot see, and find it very hard to believe in, jurisdictions that exist in the minds of a people. We need some form of political tourism; we need to be able to visit an office, to watch a debate, to make a journey that is guided by the language of hierarchical authority. We need to ask questions. The hunting and trapping peoples of the north, on the contrary, need to be able to vest their authority in themselves as individuals and to share both the knowledge and produce that the knowledge generates to ensure that their system, their families and individuals, will survive into the future. They need to be able to move freely, in tune with the world about them and their ideas of the world within themselves. They need and respect knowledge, but use it without subordinacy. Their collectivity is vital to them, as are their lands and beliefs. But the richness of their lands, the efficacy of their beliefs and the health of the collective all depend on the absence of formal, limiting, confusing institutions. For northern peoples, egalitarian individualism is at the heart of social integrity and wellbeing.

Chapter 8

Children

*

All people have a desire
for continuity of themselves in the
future. That is why people have families, so they can pass
on to their children their values and their own way of
relating to the world, so that their children
can continue as they had before them.

Steve Kakfwi
Fort Good Hope

I have my grandmother's name,
my mother's mother; she was Tagurnaaq.
Louis Tapatai marries my mother.
He calls Tagurnaaq Mother-in-law. So here I am,
also called Tagurnaaq. Naturally my father calls me
Mother-in-law and I call him Son-in-law, because my
mother is my daughter, daughter of Tagurnaaq,
and she calls me Mother.

Armand Tagurnaaq
Baker Lake

*

When an Inuit baby is a few days old it is given its *atiq*. This *atiq*, usually translated as name, constitutes an essence or soul (though we must imagine away the Christian connotations of these terms in order to translate with accuracy). This 'soul', however, is someone else. Among most Inuit, the newborn's *atiq* is an old relative who has died, frequently a grandparent or great-uncle or aunt. For the rest of its life, those who do not know the child will ask: '*Kinamik atirqarpit?*', 'whom do you have as an *atiq?*'

Many Inuit say that they can recall events that took place before they were born. Life in the womb is not set apart from life after birth. One old woman has recounted what she claims are her experiences of life in the womb, including a memory of its entrance-way, through which a 'dog' periodically inserted its head and neck, and vomited. Only later in her life did the woman realize she had been seeing her father's penis and ejaculation. In Sanikiluaq, an elderly man has recalled seeing the inside of his white father's cabin while his Inuit mother visited there before he was born. Nonetheless, until a child receives an *atiq*, it is not a complete person. This may help to explain the seemingly para-doxical association in Inuit culture of intensely passionate feel-ing for children and occasional infanticide at birth. This practice, like the assisted suicide of ailing elders, has been wildly exaggerated in popular literature about the Inuit. However, at times and in areas where the birth of a new child is a grave prob-lem, infanticide has occurred. It could not be done to a child with an *atiq*.

Once given its *atiq*, every child is both him- or herself and someone whom its parents want to immortalize. The infant is also an adult, loved for itself and for being an admired and be-loved member of an older generation.

Among the Dene and Cree, newborn babies are examined to discover who has been reincarnated: birthmarks, mannerisms, physical traits may identify who the child was in a previous life. Sometimes no evidence is found until many years later: it is not uncommon for teenagers suddenly to discover, perhaps in a vision or dream, perhaps by recognizing the possessions or campsites they used in another life, who they once were and – in an important sense – really are.

The perpetuation of the *atiq* among the Inuit and belief in reincarnation among Dene and Cree ensure the continuity of culture and are a denial of death. The wisest and most loved members of the society, repositories of ancient knowledge and guarantors of cultural identity, cannot be allowed to disappear.

In securing the immortality of the wisest and most loved, these beliefs also mean that no child is only a child, and feelings for and behaviour towards children are shaped by feelings and behaviour in relation to some of the most respected elders. If I give my grandfather's *atiq* to my baby daughter, she *is* my grandfather. I will call her *ataatassiaq*, grandfather. She is entitled to call me grandson. Can I scold her? Could I tell my grandfather he ought to be in bed? Could I instruct my grandfather to finish his breakfast? These are possibilities that arise in cultures where children are not regarded as authorities on their own needs. Among the hunting people of the north, however, where the distinction between needs and wants is not conceded, both baby and grandfather can decide when they want to go to bed, what they do and do not want to eat. The scolding of either child or elder is felt to be intrusive and wrong.

Among the Inuit, intelligence or rationality is translated as *isuma* or *ihuma* (in some dialects *s* becomes *h*). Anyone who is short-tempered is said to have insufficient *isuma*; a young person who disregards the preferences of his parents is likewise said to be lacking in *isuma*; a hunter who sets off on a journey when conditions are not propitious is thought to need more *isuma*; if a

139

three-year-old misbehaves he might be asked, 'Are you failing to use your *isuma?*'

Isuma, however, is not thought to be something that can be learned by or taught to children. Rather, it grows irrespective of intellectual or moral influences imposed upon the child. Gentle steering, example, heredity – all these *are* said to influence *isuma*. But, as the anthropologist Jean Briggs observed on the basis of her work in the central Canadian Arctic, 'There is no point in trying to teach a child [*isuma*] before he shows signs of possessing it.' Inuit thus treat rationality as they would the hair on a person's head: it will develop at its own time, in its own way. Shouting at a bald baby will not make its hair appear any sooner; angry protest at childish misbehaviour will not result in good behaviour.

Inuit beliefs and ideals of human behaviour thus mean that direct disciplining of children would be both immoral and point-less. Also, when possible, children are granted what they demand. They know what they need. This feature of permissive-ness, however, has two facets. On the one hand, a child who asks to be picked up and cuddled would not be rejected. On the other hand, a child who has a tantrum on the floor is left to cry by itself – to rush over, unasked, and gather the child into your arms would be intrusive.

Humour, consistency and example – shown by peers as well as parents – seem to achieve a high degree of discipline, self-reliance and psychological wellbeing among the young in nor-thern hunting societies. Children grow up fast. Nine- or ten-year-olds are expected to play their part in the round of act-ivities, both in the home and on the land. Fourteen-year-olds work alongside their parents and are relied upon to sew, take care of vital equipment, fish, trap and hunt. Before modern schooling extended the period of childhood and brought a host of pressures to bear on ways of raising children, young men and women would enter marriages of varying degrees of formality by

the time they were twenty.

Among the hunting peoples of the Canadian north there are no rites of passage. Individuals grow at their own pace, taking their place in the society as they are able. Passage to sexual or social maturity is not marked by any ceremony, neither is there anything like a wedding transaction. Social and personal life is informal and improvisational; individuals follow their own trails. The culture and land impose their disciplines from within, establishing both consciousness and limits that are shared as knowledge and experienced as laws. The force and inevitability of these do not seem to require codes, institutions or organized ceremonies.*

Viewed through the European eyes of travellers and ethnographers who first described the far north, absence of formal institutions and codified law means that children of the Arctic grow up in a state of unconstrained freedom. Yet this freedom – as most of the early writers about the north observed – in no way prevents children from attaining an early and disciplined maturity.

Missionaries set up schools for Subarctic and Arctic boys and girls in the 1940s and 1950s. These were residential and authoritarian. Many of today's adults recall having been beaten or in other ways punished with disturbing severity for speaking their own languages. Many also recall the extreme despair they felt at

---

* In the western Arctic and along the north Pacific coast, in Alaska, eastern Siberia and northern British Columbia, a number of hunting societies are concentrated in more or less permanent communities. These include the Inupiaq whaling peoples. Strikingly, among these hunters there are rites of passage, institutionalized ceremonies and quite formal social rules. This is a function of social permanence. Similarly, Athapaskan groups, including the Carrier, Tahltan and Wet'suwet'en, living close to peoples of the North Pacific Coast, use the potlatch or feasting institutions with highly organized ways of affirming and enforcing law. Among the hunters of the Canadian north, on the other hand, social life is mobile and necessarily fluid. Here, the very fluidity allows an alternative, non-ceremonial and informal kind of social organization.

being separated from their families and homes for nine months of each year. The Canadian government established a few residential and many day schools in northern settlements in the 1950s and 1960s. Hundreds of Inuit and Indian families moved from bush camps, or adjusted their seasonal round of activities, in order not to be separated from their children. By the early 1970s, virtually every northern child attended a school where the language of instruction was English, and the curriculum – with the exception of a few hours per week of 'cultural inclusion' when elders taught sled-building and boot-sewing or told stories – came from the southern Canadian grade school system.

Inuit babies still receive their *atiq* a few days after birth. Dene and Cree children are examined in hopes of identifying who has returned. Among the Inuit and most Athapaskans and Algonquians, young parents who have been through the school system speak to their children in their own languages. Functional bilingualism in the far north is widespread. In the western Subarctic, however, the missionary and educational endeavour has reaped its reward: some young adults are unable or unwilling to speak their own language, and their children are being brought up with only English. At the same time, young people who have experienced the demands of agencies of change are most articulate in their understanding of and opposition to southern Canadian and governmental purposes.

Outsiders taking children into frightening, foreign schools caused great suffering. Based as it was on southern conviction that aboriginal peoples were not able to raise children properly, this policy also inflicted humiliation. But government educational programmes sought to prepare young people for a completely new world. And many northern parents sensed that everyone must arm themselves for change. Elders sometimes say that their children have had to learn the Canadian way in order to fight for the peoples' rights, and to resist the expropriation of their lands and culture. Sometimes these elders speak as if it has

been necessary to sacrifice much, including their relationships with their own children, to secure the kind of life and future in which they believe.

A bitter irony of modern relations between parents and children in many parts of the Canadian north lies in a generation gap that represents parental loss of influence over children at precisely the time when parents most need to depend on their children's new-found skills – skills that elders hope will protect the society according to their principles. Many now say they have indeed benefited from schooling, and that without skills in English and experience of southern culture, they would be completely unable to oppose changes that undermine their ways of life. Discontinuity is accepted as a price for continuity. For people who love their children with such passion, and treat them with respect that is underpinned by so many fundamental beliefs, this has been a terrible price to pay.

Language

ᑕᑯᕆ�

Notice

1. ᐃᔪᕋᓂᑦ ᑲᑕᓚᕞᐊᑦᑦ ᐃᓐᑦᓄᑦ

PLEASE TAKE ALL
BOOTS OFF WHEN ENTERING

2. ᔾᓪ ᐊᓂᕞᐊᑦᑦ ᕝᑎᑦᑲᑕᓚᔪ ᑕᒺ

TAKE HONEYBUCKET OUT
EVERYTIME IT'S HALF FULL

3. ᓂᓚᐅᑎᕞᑦ ᐊᓚᔪ ᐃᐅᐅᓐᑦ
ᕁᓕᖅᕞᐊᕞᑦ ᓂᓚᕝᕆᓂᑕᒺ

CLEAN ALL KITCHENWARE
AFTER EACH MEAL

4. ᐱᕁᕆᐊᕝᑲᖄᒺᕝᑦᕙᕝ: ᕁᓚᓄᑎᕝᐊᑉᕝ ᑕ᠎

ᐃᔪ **MOST IMPORTANT:**
KEEP THE BUILDING CLEAN

THE MANAGEMENT.

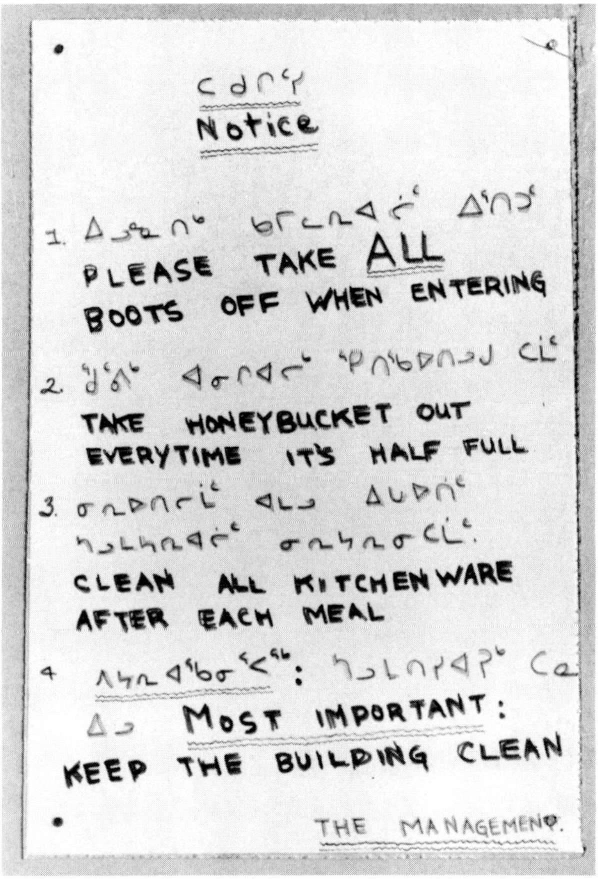

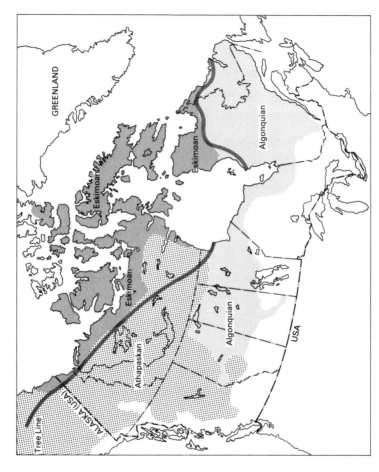

6. *Language families of the Cana-dian north*

Three language families are found in the Canadian north. These are Eskimoan, spoken by the Inuit, Athapaskan, spoken by the Dene, and Algonquian, spoken by the Cree, Naskapi and Montagnais. These three linguistic groups have very little in common: structure and vocabulary differ from one another as completely as do English, Hungarian and Cantonese. Linguists divide Algonquian into two sets of dialects, Cree and Ojibwa. The variation among them is surprisingly small. The Athapaskan language family contains twenty-three different languages. The Eskimoan language is part of the larger Eskimo–Aleut linguistic group. Eskimo can be divided into Yupik, a group of five languages, and Inuktitut–Inupiaq, a continuum of ap-proximately six dialects spread across Canada.

Inuk is the Eskimo word for a person. There are two plural forms: *inuuk*, two persons, and *inuit*, three or more persons. *Inuit* is the people's own word for themselves, and is usually (though rather misleadingly) translated as human beings or the real people. *Inuktitut* is the Inuit word for the language, and is made up of the root *inuk*, a person, with the affix *titut*, in the manner of.

This seemingly simple word has its own cultural implications. Inuit use it to mean how they speak; it also refers to the way in which they do things. A person can talk, hunt, walk, eat, sleep, raise children, dance and even smile *inuktitut*. Everything the Inuit do is revealed in their manner of doing it. A distinct identity is bound up as much in the details of everyday behaviour as in the use of language.

Inuktitut has no genders, no specific grammatical endings that distinguish between he, she and it. These can, of course, be signalled in pronouns, but their absence from nouns and verb forms suggests the equality of human beings. Not even Inuktitut personal names are gender-specific: there is no such thing as a boy's as opposed to a girl's name.

On the other hand, Inuktitut makes a multitude of precise distinctions when it comes to descriptions of space. There, above your eye level and visible; there, below your eye level and not visible; there, above your eye level and not visible; there, close to you and visible; these here; those there. A complete list of all the exact terms for locating objects in space would be extremely long.

Aboriginally, Inuktitut had no words for thank you, hello or goodbye. Such expressions imply a mixture of posturing and intrusiveness that are at odds with northern hunters' ideals of interpersonal behaviour. Newcomers to the far north are often taken aback by the way in which Inuit men and women visit and

151

leave one another's houses without any spoken formality. In fact, this reveals insistence upon and recognition of the right to do as you wish without repeatedly implicating others. Under pressure from newcomers' customs, Inuktitut had to find an equivalent for the routine English question, 'How are you?' or 'How do you do?'. The word *quanuippit?* is the most widespread result. It means 'What has gone wrong for you?' For the Inuit, the need to ask the question must be based on some evidence of a difficulty.*

There are two ways in Inuktitut of saying perhaps. One of these, *imaqa*, in effect means probably not. The other, the infix *-qu-*, means probably. Inuit rarely make statements of any importance – especially about hunting and their movements – without employing one or other of these expressions. Persons raised with European planning and certainties have great difficulty in interpreting these uses of perhaps. But the two ways of expressing the possible speak volumes about hunters' consciousness.

The addition of infixes or affixes to root words is the basis of Inuktitut structure. It is a highly agglutinative language: whole sentences can be formed by building a series of affixes on to one root. For example, the Inuit can say 'he was not allowed to hunt for caribou' with a single word, *tuttusiurqujaulaungituq*.† For those

---

* Athapaskans have borrowed *marsai* from the French *merci* for thank you.

† This breaks down as: *tuttu* – caribou; *siur* – hunt for; *qu* – instruct, permit; *jau* – indicates passive mode; *lau* – indicates past tense; *ngi* – not the case that; *tuq* – he, she, it.

The most important rule for the building of long sentence-like words is that each affix modifies everything that precedes it. This is much the same as the use of brackets in mathematics or formal logic: in an Inuktitut word in which a root x is modified by a, d and j and so is constructed $xadj$, the mathematical notation expressing the logical relation between the items would be: $j(d[a\{x\}])$, i.e. j modifies all that lies between the round brackets, d modifies all that lies between the square brackets and a all between the curly brackets, namely x, the root. Thus, in the example about not being allowed to hunt caribou, the negative, *ngi*, modifies the sum of the expression that precedes it, and not just the *lau*, the past tense indicator. It follows that the pronoun or person is usually the final element.

interested in sounding this correctly it is important to know that *q* is used for a short, guttural *k*; try beginning 'cow' at the back of the throat. There are two other sounds in some eastern Arctic dialects that present problems for Europeans: a fricative *l*, familiar to anyone who has tried to pronounce Welsh names that begin with *ll*, and a rounded *r* sound that is like trying to pronounce *r* and *j* at the same time, as if trying to say 'regent' without the first *e*. Apart from these unfamiliar consonants, English speakers can easily learn to pronounce Inuktitut. Inuit themselves sometimes observe that French and German speakers have little difficulty with Inuktitut sounds.*

A feature of Inuktitut is its regularity. There are virtually no exceptions to its rules. The combination of precise agglutination with these clear logical principles means that Inuktitut has a remarkable capacity to deal with new notions and terms. So long as an imported expression or loan word is given an Inuktitut ending, it can be declined, conjugated and modified within the Inuktitut system.

Modern Inuktitut dialects reveal some incorporation of other languages. In Labrador, for example, where German-speaking Moravian missionaries were the first newcomers to influence the language, many Inuktitut loan words are obviously from the German. These include the words for week (*wurik* from *Woche*), year (*jaarik* from *Jahr*), the way of telling the time and some numbers (*ainsili, tsuvailik, turai* from *ein, zwei, drei*). In these cases, the Labrador Inuit adopted German forms for words that already existed in Inuktitut, and modern Labrador Inuit use both forms. In other cases, where new things required new words, German loan words were adapted to fit the Labrador dialect. An example

---

* Algonquian presents few pronunciation difficulties to Europeans, whereas Athapaskan, from the point of view of both pronunciation and grammar, is extremely challenging to speakers of European languages. The Athapaskanist James Kari has said that it requires as much as ten years to develop a working facility in any Athapaskan language.

of this is *kartupalak*, potato, from the German *Kartoffel*. In most dialects, this kind of borrowing is from English, so we find *tii* (tea), *kaapi* (coffee) and *palauga* (flour). The elaborate possibilities for agglutination also mean that Inuktitut terms can be combined to make new words. Modern Inuktitut abounds with such new expressions. Many go back to early contact with newcomers, but others are of recent origin. Older words include:

niaquujak (resembles a head)	bread
qianattuq (causes tears)	onion
naitingujarvik (time that resembles taboo-observance)	Sunday
kiinaujak (resembles a face)	money
imuksiutik (thing for milk)	cow
kuviasukvik (happiness occasion or place)	Christmas

Newer words include:

nunakuurutik (device for going by land)	car
qangatasuuk (persistently soars)	aeroplane
irqiasulaaktigijutik (device that makes you curly)	hair curler
mamaksautik (thing that makes tasty)	perfume (Ungava) ketchup (N. Baffin)
ujaraksiurvik (place for looking for rock)	mine
uksualuk (great, extreme blubber)	petrol/oil
uksualungniartik (one who attends to great blubber)	oil company
inulirijik (one who fixes up people)	northern administrator
aijuksakturlirijik (one who fixes up ones who may be in difficulty)	welfare officer/ social worker

We took some kids out camping.
When we told them to get firewood, they cut down
live trees instead of dead ones. They did not understand
the word for dry wood . . .
Some of our children are learning French in school;
others learn English. Maybe that is good. If they want to
talk to each other, they will have to continue speaking
Inuktitut.

Peter Morgan
George River

I told the boy, *iglaisillutit*, untangle the
dogs' leads. He stared at me. He said, I don't
have a comb with me. He thought I was asking him to
comb his hair. It's the same word. He had
not learned its real meaning.

Isaac Amituq
Sanikiluaq

Somebody dies and the name goes to a baby, it does not
matter whether it is a boy or a girl.

Catherine Arnatisiaq
Igloolik

*

Language

The languages of northern hunters are rich and precise. Never having relied on written texts, great care is taken when speaking to ensure that exact meaning is understood. As is the case in all oral cultures, conventions that guide the way in which people listen are no less rigorous than those that shape speaking styles. Someone who is telling a story or reflecting upon events can take it for granted that he or she will not be interrupted. As a result, the spoken language is slow, exploratory, often somewhat discursive and almost completely lacking the equivalent of English *ers* and *ums*. Also, anyone coming from a European-speaking tradition cannot help being struck by the way in which northern hunters speak without using gestures to emphasize or reflect their meanings and moods. Language is relied upon to do the real work.

A feature of all three language groups is their lack of generic terms. In Inuktitut, for example, there is no word for seal or fish. A speaker must identify particular species. Similarly, Athapaskan languages have no word for grouse; a hunter must indicate which of the several kinds of grouse he or she is talking about.

Specificity of language is a useful indicator of what language loss can mean. Under Euro-Canadian influence, modern Inuit use the work *iqaluk*, sea-going arctic char, to mean fish. Similarly, many northern Athapaskans use chicken to mean all species of grouse. Thus, when speaking English Dunne-za will refer to chicken, but in their own language will distinguish between spruce, ruffed and sharp-tailed grouse (*chi'djo, chicha* and *chis'konste*). Many white northerners use *natiq*, ringed seal, to mean seal. And when speaking English Inuit refer to seals, whereas in Inuktitut they speak of ringed seal, harp seal, bearded seal or harbour seal (*natiq, kairulik, ujjuk* or *qasigiak*). Presumably, a Dunne-za who speaks only English may see only chicken instead of the various species of grouse. Loss of language can constitute not only a reduction in knowledge but an impoverishment of the observed – of experience itself.

159

ᐱᐅᓚᓴᐅᓯᒪᖕᒋᑐᑦ
ᐃᒪᖅᓯᒪᔪᑎᑐᑦ-ᐃᐳᑦ

149

Softly And Tenderly

1. ᓇᒃᑕᒍᓱᒃᑯᓂ ᑮᕐᑯᕐᓯᑕᖅᐳᖅ
ᐃᓕᖕᓂᒃ ᐅᖃᒪᓂᒃᑯ,
ᑭᓄᐃᖅᑳᕐᑯᓂ ᐅᑕᕐᑭᑕᖅᐳᖅ
ᐃᓕᖕᓂᒃ ᐅᖃᒪᓂᒃᑯ.

2. ᐱᐅᓚᓴᖅᑐᕋᕕᖓ
ᐊᔪᕐᓂᓇᓴᒃᑲ,
ᑲᐸᐱᐊᒋᓴᒃᑲ..
ᐃᓕᖕᓄᑦ ᐱᑎᐸᐸᒃᑲ..
ᐲᓴᓚᐅᒃᑭᑦ ᑐᕐᑯᖕᓄᑦ
ᐄᓕᖕᖓ ᐃᑭᖕᓄᑦ.

3. ᐸᓯᓴᒃᓴᐅᒐᖕᒐ
ᐊᐅᑦ ᑯᕕᓚᐅᕋᕕᐅᒃ,
ᐆᒧᖕᒐ ᐃᕐᕿᕐᒥᖕᒐ..
ᒪᓂᒍᕿᒃ ᐃᓗᒐ..
ᐊᔪᕐᓂᒃᑲ ᑕᒣᑕ
ᐃᕐᑲᐅᒪᔪᖕᓅᕐᓗᒋᑦ.

Tribal peoples' languages are often said to be primitive. In fact, the grammar of isolated languages tends to be richer than that of languages which have experienced outside linguistic influences. Encounters between grammars often result in grammatical simplification. For example, in Inuktitut there are two plural forms, a dual and a three-or-more. Inuit who speak English, however, and are familiar with the simpler division into singular and plural, tend to abandon the Inuktitut dual form. And we have already seen that richness of vocabulary can be eroded by innovative simplification.

A more persistent, popular charge against aboriginal languages is that they are paramountly concrete, that they cannot cope with abstract ideas and that peoples who speak them are not able to participate in debates about the future of their lands and society. In fact, Inuktitut can create abstractions with great ease. The infix *na*, when inserted after either verb or noun forms, establishes a disposition or an 'ism' rather like the German affix *-keit*. Thus, in Inuktitut *anniatuq* means it hurts; *anniarnattuq* means painful. That is a simple and translatable abstraction. But, using the same infix, the word for wearing a shirt, *uvinurutuq*, can be turned into an abstract concept, *uvinurunattuq*, whose meaning is hard to render in English. It is something like a tendency towards or disposition for shirts. The difficulty of translation here, however, in no way reflects a problem for Inuktitut speakers; for them, the abstraction generated by the *na* would be automatically intelligible. If some terms are not to be found in Inuktitut, it is because they have so far not been coined. 'Relativism' is no harder to render in Inuktitut than 'kangaroo': neither has, but both could become, part of the language.

Inuit received an orthography, adapted by missionaries from a writing system used to translate the Bible among northern Algonquian peoples in the late nineteenth century. This, the Inuit script, is a syllabic orthography, easy to learn but very

tue dih gah

f	f	f	t u e
f	f	t u e	f
t u e	f	f	f
f	f	t u e	f
f	t u e	t u e	
f	f	f	t u e
f	t u e	f	f
t u e	f	f	f

m m	d i h	m m
d i h	m d i	h
m d i	h m m	m
m m m	d i h	m
d i h	m m m	m
d i h	m m m	m
m m m	d i h	m
m d i	h m m	m
m m m m	d i h	

k	g a h	k k	k
g a h	k	g a h	
k k k	g a h	k	
k	g a h	k k	k
g a h	k k	k	k
k k k	g a h	k	
g a h	k	g a h	
k g a h	k k	k	
k k k k	g a h		

imprecise and therefore usable only by persons who are more or less fluent in the language. Nevertheless, syllabics spread fast across the eastern Canadian Arctic, where isolated communities learned it from neighbours to the south. Some Inuit, therefore, were literate before any white missionaries reached them. In Greenland, a Roman orthography was used for the Greenlandic Eskimo during the early days of Danish administration. And in Siberia, first a Cyrillic and then a Roman orthography was developed in the 1920s for Yuit, the eastern Siberian Eskimoan group. But in the Canadian Arctic, the only writings available to Inuit in the 1960s were parts of the Bible, a book of common prayer and a small number of government leaflets explaining various social welfare programmes.

In fact, colonial agencies – with the possible exception of missions – have imposed English upon peoples across the north. Those who have learned the aboriginal languages have usually done so to effect changes that would make the people more like themselves. And, in recent times, most southerners who move to the north would never think that they could or should learn an indigenous language. Instead, the working assumption of new agencies has been that, with time and effort, all northern people will come to speak English. Attitude to local languages is a major indicator of how cultures view one another. In Canada this is reflected in the limited nature of available written materials. Comparison with other countries is also revealing. In Greenland, nineteenth-century literature – including such classics as *Jane Eyre* – was translated into Greenlandic Eskimo. In 1966 fifty-eight books, totalling over 56,000 copies, were available in Siberian Eskimo. The Siberian books included a mathematics textbook of high-school level.

The Siberian and Greenlandic evidence shows that Arctic languages are not limited or limiting in ways that would justify their displacement by English. The Canadian slowness to provide written materials, therefore, is a result of larger, broadly

political forces. English was seen by many as the language of civilization, and by others as the facilitator of administration. Nonetheless, northern hunting peoples themselves have sought to retain their languages, and in many cases adapted them to new purposes. The Dene of the Mackenzie Valley, when negotiating their first land-claim proposals, insisted on bringing a group of elders, speakers exclusively of Athapaskan, to participate in and advise at all negotiating sessions. More recently, the Northwest Territories government became an elected instead of a delegated administration, as a result of which the Inuit and Dene found themselves in a position of majority control. They immediately implemented a thoroughgoing translation programme, both in the Council Chamber and across the Northwest Territories as a whole. They also pursued a policy of education in aboriginal languages for the first three grades of schooling in Dene villages in the Northwest Territories.

Programmes of this kind have shown that even northern Athapaskan languages can be written and take their place among modern literatures and in school curricula. With at least forty consonants, nine vowels and three tones (high, low and rising pitch), these would seem to defy simplified European orthography and language abilities. But writing systems have been devised in Alaska, Yukon and the Northwest Territories. In the 1980s, books have been published and used in schools.* At Rae Edzo in the western Arctic, a Dene teacher discovered that Dene children learned to write more quickly if taught to do so in their own language. The limitations placed upon northern languages, therefore, are a feature of outside pressures; the languages themselves have the same possibilities as all others – in the north, for which they are finely tuned and superbly expressive, far more so. In fact, Inuktitut continues to be the first language for some 80 per cent of all Inuit homes. Among Naskapi the percentage who

* See bibliography for some of the titles.

165

speak their own language is even higher. Among Athapaskans and Cree it is smaller and varies considerably from region to region. But in virtually every northern community, there is a strong reliance upon the native language.

Nonetheless, all northern languages are under great pressure. Most schooling continues to be in English. In Arctic Quebec, a small number of villages have French schools. Training local persons to be teachers and the use of classroom assistants who speak to children in their own languages play their part in the northern educational programme. But it is a small part. To match northern to southern curricula remains the objective of Canadian educational policy. This leaves little space within northern schooling for the special circumstances of the Subarctic and Arctic regions. The strengths, knowledge and confidence that depend upon fluency in one's own language are still at risk.

Chapter 10

'Tradition'

Do Inuit live in snow houses? Do they travel by dog team? Do they hunt seals with harpoons? Do they move about, from camp to camp, in a round of seasonal activities? Do they eat raw meat? Do they dry fish in the sun? Do they make *igunaaq*, 'high' meat? Do they wear caribou-skin clothing? Do they speak of weather as the presence of Sila, the air spirit? Do the Dene track moose through the woods on foot? Do they use snares and deadfalls? Do they believe and follow a shamanistic spirituality? Do they think that muskrat played an important role in the creation of the earth? Do Naskapi follow the caribou herds, far inland? Do they dream their way through time? Do they travel in dreams? Do they have summer gathering grounds? Do the Cree move on to winter trapping grounds each year? Do they rely on snowshoes to move through the bush? Do they make hunting cabins each season, and lay spruce boughs as mattresses? Do they make medicines from herbs and roots? Do they use medicine power in spiritual life? Do they trap beaver under the winter ice? Do Innu prepare skins on stretcher frames and boards? Do they depend on the fur trade? Do they wear moccasins? Do they prepare dry meat each autumn as a supply of concentrated protein for the coming seasons? Are children seen as elders reborn?

A simple answer to all these questions is yes.

Do northern hunting peoples live in prefabricated houses, provided by the Canadian government? Are they concentrated in settlements, where social services and administrators reach into almost every corner of their lives? Do they get drunk a lot? Do they speak English? Do men work as labourers for the oil and gas industry? Do the people go to church? Do hunters hurry to and from their hunting grounds on snowmobiles? Do they use high-powered rifles and telescopic sights? Do Inuit have refrigerators? Do Innu have televisions? Do Cree have stereo systems? Do

Dene drive pick-up trucks? Do Naskapi wear jeans? Are the young confused and angry? Are northern hunting peoples dependent on cash and the local supermarket? Do they look to southern doctors and drugs for medical help? Do the old receive state pensions?

A simple answer to all these questions is yes.

But how can people use dog teams as well as snowmobiles? How can they live in both snow houses and prefabricated bungalows? How can they depend upon both the harpoon and the rifle? How can they be both shamanistic and Christian? How can they exist, at one and the same time, in the past and the present?

It is all too easy for us to express incredulity, and even indignation, over these seeming inconsistencies. Discussion and opinion about aboriginal peoples take much of their shape from our preconception of the traditional, and a sense that proper and unquestionable evolution of human societies is from simplicity to complexity, from primitive happiness and poverty to modern alienation and riches. Traditional life loses its force, its very being, if violated by the modern. We feel great disappointment when we discover that those whom we expect to be traditionalists turn out to drive pick-up trucks. At the same time we hear these very people talking loudly about special rights. They seem not to be content with ordinary Canadian administration and schools; they want royalties from mineral extraction; they want assured incomes for hunters. If only they – and the whole Third World – would get modernized quickly, we feel, that would surely solve their problems. Why can't they make up their minds to be either traditional or modern? Either they should live like us, and take their inconspicious place within the general melting pot, or they should live in genuine, aboriginal isolation within reserve lands.

And so we force a moral choice upon aboriginal peoples. We consign them to one of two possible categories: traditional or

modern. They must be one or the other. We challenge and reproach them with the question: do you belong in the past or the present? Hunters who rely on rifles are sneered at by romantic purists who believe that only a hunter with harpoon or bow and arrows is really a hunter. Hunters who insist on using worn and battered .30/30s are despised for failure to understand the advantages of the telescopic sight. Men and women wearing wool trousers and down parkas are scorned for 'failing' to rely on caribou- and moose-hide clothing. People who do wear skin clothing are looked down on as backward or romanticized as representatives of the stone age. Indians in the bar are dismissed as degenerates. Inuit who encourage their children to spend time on the land rather than in school are warned that they are jeopardizing the next generation's best prospects. Inuit who collect welfare payments are felt to have let down both us and themselves.

This imposition of a traditional–modern dichotomy is irrational. All people live in both the past and the present. To have parents, to care about your home, to make use of the land and its resources, to exist in society – these all require that we have one foot firmly in the past, even for those who embrace modernity with unambiguous passion. All human cultures seek to realize and protect their identity. And identity is definable only by reference to former times. Our commitment to the past is often unconscious or symbolic; it is nonetheless integral to who we are and how we live. Even in North America, where disavowal of the past has sometimes been pursued as a principle of existence in what is rightly called 'the New World', modernity cannot exist of and for itself. All individuals and communities have traditions and histories of which they are proud.

We do not decide whether we are going to exist in the past or the present. We may laugh, or even sneer, at the old-fashioned in our own societies, but we do not criticize one another for failing to *choose* between the old and the new. We do not impale our-

175

selves or our society on the horns of a traditional versus modern dilemma. This means that we judge hunting peoples, along with most other aboriginal peoples, by standards we do not apply to ourselves.

Why is this? Why are so many Europeans and North Americans eager to impose this unreal choice upon hunting cultures?

One result of the industrial revolution has been that the old seem to be less competent, even less experienced, than the young. The latest technological discoveries – microchips and electronics, in particular – have reinforced with new intensity a sense in urban culture that the young understand more than the old. This may explain some of the impatience and misapprehension that shape Euro-American judgements of tribal cultures in general, and hunting societies in particular: for them, age, and therefore the past, is a mixture of bank and library, a vital resource for the present and future. At the same time, urban peoples are aware of the price they pay for modern advantages: pollution, alienation, war. Perhaps this causes a demand that other, non-urban, 'traditional' peoples must take it or leave it; the idea that they might select the bits of modernity that suit their purposes, while rejecting the unpleasant concomitants, irritates us. We are jealous of their seeming freedom, and wish to deny it them.

Perhaps the answer lies, therefore, in the alienation experienced in Euro-American societies. We may feel that modernity has broken our spiritual lives and caused a separation from the real. We may imagine that in other kinds of society relations between people and animals, people and the land, people and people, humans and gods, are harmonious. We may feel that aboriginal cultures know (or knew) how to avoid the abrasive and discordant dealings that have led our world to self-destruction. With these thoughts and needs in mind, perhaps we look to tribal peoples for a model of another, better form of existence. Consciousness of the failings of Western culture thus might

spawn romantic expectations of other cultures. And when we find that the hunter is drunk, or in church, or racing across the sea ice on his snowmobile, we are disappointed and indignant. They are not doing what we need them to do; they are not an embodiment of a traditional life that may offer some sort of last hope for mankind.

Confusion surrounding the traditional–modern dichotomy can be seen in the way northern peoples have entered international handicraft and art markets. Men and women in hunting societies are all skilful and creative in their making, mending and ornamenting of everyday equipment and clothing. They also make toys for children and carve stone to represent animals and characters from their oral histories and shamanistic stories. In the 1950s and 1960s, many of these skills were directed into producing clothing and works of art for southern markets. As a result, Inuit became famous for soapstone figurines and prints; Subarctic Indians became known for beaded moccasins, tassled jackets and dolls. But demand was for 'primitive' art and 'traditional' handicrafts. This meant that saleable subject matter was restricted to scenes that evoked the buyers' idea of how the north should look and northern peoples should think: this new art market grew on images of 'traditional' life. At the same time, many carvers have been anxious to affirm their distinct heritage, and have expressed this in their repeated use of 'traditional' images. The peoples' political fears, their wish to affirm the importance of hunting and trapping, and southern buyers' romantic tastes coincided. This helps to explain the power and success of the work. Beautiful as much of the new art is, however, it comes from confining the artists' imaginations. A small number of men and women have broken from this constraint. Tiktak of Rankin Inlet has produced a series of abstract works in stone. Some younger men and women have depicted snowmobiles and rifles. But as a whole, the new art of this far north has become a folksy entrapment of the old. It has provided a steady cash eco-

*

I like walking in the water,
and watching seals. I like going hunting,
going on a speedboat. I like going dancing,
but best of all I like to fish.

Katie Zarpa
Nain

For means of transportation on lakes and rivers
they use canoes with outboard motors, and no longer
paddle ... In summary, the Indians and Inuit have abandoned
the way of life of their ancestors and have adopted
that of the whites.

Mr Justice Turgeon
Appeal Courts, Quebec, 1973

We will always see ourselves as part of nature.
Whether we use outboard motors or plywood for our cabins
does not make us any less Indian ... We are Indians just
like our fathers and grandfathers, and just like
our children and grandchildren
will be.

Richard Nerysoo
Fort McPherson

*

nomy, but is a denial of the modern, an obscuring of the peoples' real lives.

Our harsh judgement against hunters who fail to be traditional also serves a rather more mundane material purpose. We associate the strength of tradition, the survival of tribal culture and continuing reliance on subsistence activities with moral and legal rights to the land. If the peoples of the north continue to live off resources they have harvested and protected for millennia, who can possibly say that those resources belong to someone else? And if those hunters are content, healthy and clear in their attachment to their own way of living, who can say that colonial settlement or industrial transformation will improve their lot? North American society and economy, however, are based on the expropriation and transformation of tribal peoples. The forward momentum of that society, therefore, requires the continuing denial of peoples' rights. The traditional–modern dichotomy assists in this denial, for it establishes a basis for concluding that the people who originally used and owned the land no longer benefit from it, or fail to make the right kind of use of it.

Thus the judgement that we tend to make about northern hunting peoples serves the purposes of an expanding, internal imperialism. We insist that they have espoused the modern and rejected the old, and therefore have no right to oppose mines, oil and gas pipelines or whatever development serves North American frontier purposes. We say that they have abandoned their way of life, and therefore they have no right to insist upon it. We say that they are caught in a cultural twilight, lost between two worlds, therefore they can only benefit from a rapid and more or less complete assimilation. The economic and political advantages of the traditional–modern dichotomy are not difficult to discern.

However, the hunting peoples of the north, along with many tribal and aboriginal groups around the world, reject the dichotomy. Throughout their entire history, and with special intensity

since Europeans reached their lands, they have chosen to adopt new items of material and intellectual culture. They use dog teams and snowmobiles because in some places and for some things the dog team is better, while in others the snowmobile has advantages and – at least for the time being – has taken over as the primary means of hunting and transport. In Igloolik and Hall Beach, for example, hunting parties are sometimes composed of families travelling by dog team and skidoo. The two methods complement each other. There is protection against breakdown far from home; dog teams do not run out of petrol. And there is the advantage of rapid survey of breathing holes, the sea ice edge or a trapline; skidoos are faster than dog teams. In the Subarctic, Dene travel by pick-up truck to a hunting area, and then spread on foot, tracking moose or mule deer along trails and with skills that reach back to time immemorial. In all parts of the far north, hunting families live in prefabricated bungalows for much of the year, but when on hunting trips they make use of snow houses or bush shelters or tepees – the devices that allow mobility and flexibility upon which the success of the hunt continues to rely. Moreover, hunting and trapping depends on technology, wisdom and experience that are carried in the brain. It is in the complex universe of the mind, where knowledge and invention evolve unceasingly, that the old and new can meet and balance one another in ever changing patterns.

In their actual beliefs and practices hunting peoples are a blend of the old and the new, and in this way exist as our contemporaries. But to protect their lands and their right to their own form of modernity, all northern groups have had to fight for what they regard as aboriginal title to their lands and ways of life. This fight has led them to make presentations at commissions of inquiry, to conduct their own social-scientific and biological studies, to engage in complex negotiations with government departments and to argue for their rights in courts of law. In all these settings, the people have made use of every means avail-

able to them; they have employed modernity in their own defence. What they have sought to defend, however, is neither the traditional nor the modern, but their right to choose the components of their own lives.

Chapter 11

Frontiers

In 1910 Vilhjalmur Stefansson was welcomed by the Copper Eskimo of the central Arctic – a people who, Stefansson claimed, had no knowledge that any other humans existed. And it was only in 1914 that Robert Flaherty, who later became famous as a film-maker, discovered the Qiqirtarmiut living on the Belcher Islands, which, prior to Flaherty's discovery, were generally believed to be deserted, rocky offshore islets.

But the anthropological drama of such recent discoveries obscures the much more general fact that most of Canada's northern peoples came under the influence of European culture in the course of the nineteenth century, and some groups had regular contact with explorers, whalers or traders from the late seventeenth century. Even groups with no direct contact with southerners came to depend on items of southern material culture. Iron, tea, tobacco and firearms spread with or ahead of the adventurers who made it at least part of their business to convey such goods further and further north. Old men and women on the Belcher Islands recall the occasion on which they first had dealings with a southerner, but in 1972 not even the oldest islanders could remember a time when they were without a gun.

The history of the far north is the story of frontiers. Unexplored territory and untapped resources captured European imagination and fed visions of sudden riches. Region by region, economic sector by economic sector, the Subarctic and Arctic have been celebrated as a new or – in an idiom that lays claim to old romantic connections – a last frontier. Some of these frontiers have depended upon the co-operation and support of aboriginal people; for others, the Inuit, Dene, Cree, Naskapi and Innu are an obstacle in the way of the newcomers' schemes for development.

In the seventeenth and eighteenth centuries, fur traders who had established themselves along the St Lawrence moved north-

ward. All northern peoples probably heard rumours of white newcomers, and may have seen some of the new materials that Europeans had brought with them. Some, notably the James Bay Cree, became involved in the fur trade by the 1700s. But for Inuit, Dene and Naskapi, the first two centuries of American colonial presence were a distant, perhaps inaudible rumble.

In the nineteenth century, whalers discovered that Arctic coastal waters were the summer feeding grounds of many thousands of bowhead, belugas and walruses. The whale was that century's counterpart to the petroleum industry. Its oil provided illuminants and lubricants. Baleen ('whalebone') held the place of plastics in an enormous range of manufactured goods including corset stays, skirt hoops, umbrella ribs, fishing rods, riding crops, brushes, window blinds, upholstery stuffing, carriage springs, luggage and fences. To provide the essential raw material for such products, the whaling frontier advanced into the furthest recesses of High Arctic fjords and islands. Ships loaded themselves to the waterline with whale oil, baleen and walrus ivory that earned large profits on European markets.

At first, this whaling frontier proceeded with minimum dealings with the Inuit. From the whaler's point of view, Inuit visitors to the whaling boats were amusing and intriguing. From the Inuit point of view, whalers were a source of fascinating and, in some cases, valuable new goods, while the washed-up wrecks of ships that did not make it through Arctic waters or ice constituted a rich supply of iron and timber.

But in the 1850s whalers began overwintering successfully. By being present when the whales first reappeared in spring, they could double their May and June kills. One priority in selecting a wintering site was proximity of an Inuit encampment. The hunters' main contribution was to provide fresh meat throughout the winter, but they also transported blubber from the ice edge to the ship by dog sled, provided guides for hunting excursions and helped generally with spring whaling. Women made

fur clothing and sleeping bags, as well as fulfilling the role of seasonal wives below deck. The establishment of new shore stations also relied on Inuit labour and traded fur and ivory. In return, Inuit received an impressive variety of manufactured goods which, with great flexibility, they incorporated into their daily lives. By the end of the period of commercial whaling, in about 1912, hunters were using rifles, telescopes, sheath knives, jack-knives, hatchets, saws, drills, awls, steels and files. Women cooked in metal pots and kettles, and used steel needles, cotton thread and metal scissors in sewing. Summer clothing consisted of woollen shawls and long cotton skirts for women; cloth trousers, shirts, jackets, caps and even waistcoats for men, who were occasionally seen in bowler hats or nautical caps and sunglasses.

Less obvious and more or less benign results of this frontier can be seen in the music and dancing that many eastern Arctic communities now regard as part of their tradition – adapted Scottish reels and sets that were first seen on whaling ships and at whalers' shore stations. The less benign results, however, include epidemics of viral infections to which the Inuit had no immunity; in the case of the Inuvialuit of the Mackenzie Delta, a combination of new diseases resulted in the virtual extermination of the original community: from an estimated 2,000, their number fell to no more than thirty.

The Hudson's Bay Company received its charter in 1670, providing it with a monopoly position as fur traders in north-west North America. Its trade was centred in the James Bay region throughout the eighteenth century and spread into the Subarctic and Arctic in the course of the 1800s. From about 1780 to 1820, and again in the early 1900s, the Hudson's Bay Company's monopoly was challenged by French and American rivals. Despite the competition – at times aggressive and warlike – the spread of the fur trade into the far north was a protracted process, completed only by 1950. Over this long span of time and

vast extent of territory, the fur trade obviously varied greatly. But the underlying purpose of fur traders was the same everywhere. They depended upon the production of fine furs by hunters whose economic and social lives were carefully attuned to production of meat.

In some cases, northern hunters adapted quickly and, from the traders' point of view, effectively to this new frontier activity. In other cases, hunters were reluctant to change and made limited compromises with the newcomers. Elders and shamans feared that the delicate balance between human and animal movements would be disrupted by dependence on fur trade posts, and saw their influence and system of values to be in jeopardy. Many hunters had to be lured and pressured into the degree of dependence upon white newcomers and their goods or services that would ensure a readiness to trade. To this end, alcohol was offered to trappers whenever they visited the trading post: hunters may not need many European goods, but they would surely become dependent on drink. Also, in the nineteenth century, the Hudson's Bay Company economists discovered that trappers offered more furs for sale when prices were lowest, for they then could satisfy their limited need for manufactured goods only by selling large quantities of furs. Conventional supply and demand theory had to be turned on its head: prices were kept as low as possible, despite extreme fluctuation in availability of many fine fur species. Hudson's Bay Company factors imported foodstuffs and sold them below cost to keep trappers from subsistence hunting; offered jobs, but not during the winter trapping season and only to reliable trappers; provided welfare to widows, orphans, the aged and infirm; extended credit to ensure that trappers returned to their particular trading post; and insisted on a barter in their own payment units to prevent the freedom that cash would give to a trapper to choose amongst different fur buyers and suppliers of manufactured goods. The effects of the fur trade varied from time to time and place to

place, but at some levels the results for Subarctic and Arctic peoples were the same everywhere: independent hunters came to be dependent trappers.

Among the earliest cultural impacts of the fur trade was the creation of a new group of people, the Métis, at first the children of French fur traders and Cree mothers. This group became large and distinctive enough to constitute a political force in North America in the late nineteenth century and, under the leadership of Riel, mounted separatist insurrections against eastern Canadian hegemony in 1869 and 1885. Further north, a Métis group, descendants of liaisons between Scottish and English fur traders and Dene women, developed along the Mackenzie River. Northern Métis commingled easily with their Athapaskan and Algonquian relations. In the early days, Métis or half-caste children were able to act as influential middlemen by becoming interpreters or managers at trading posts. But surprisingly quickly the Métis either merged with other Indian groups or constituted a separate sub-culture of their own.

Métis culture, in fact, took several different forms. In the early days, persons of mixed Indian and settler ancestry were distinguished according both to their European and tribal background. Hence early names for Métis included Black Scots, Bois Brûlé or Burnt Wood, Métis Anglais, as well as the widespread – and often derogatory – halfbreed or breed. To some extent, this separation of Métis groups was reflected in their speaking various mixes of languages. Through the nineteenth century, however, the Métis separated into small farmers, servants to white agents and colonists, and hunters and trappers. In the Canadian far north, where virtually all land is beyond the agricultural frontier, and where twentieth-century agencies have ceased to depend on local servants and middlemen, the Métis and others of aboriginal ancestry have come to share the general social and economic points of view and interests of their neighbouring hunting peoples.

197

Dene, Inuit, Naskapi and Innu became trappers as well as hunters in the late nineteenth or early twentieth centuries. The difficulties that the transition entailed can there be seen quite clearly. Once factors had established dependence upon the posts, the people became vulnerable to any change in the conditions or flow of the goods and services that traders dispensed. Caribou hunters who decided to travel to a trading post rather than adjust their movements in relation to caribou herds could find, if the post was closed or the trader reluctant to extend credit, that they were caught between a potentially pathetic reliance on white handouts, the generosity of neighbours or a precarious attempt to move back towards the caribou over territory devoid of game. In at least one documented case, just this kind of circumstance resulted in the starvation of several whole households.

In Sanikiluaq, south Hudson Bay, as late as 1940 hunters experienced great difficulty in getting credit at a time when their changed pattern of movement and difficult ice conditions had combined to result in starvation conditions. Elders there recall that one particular family was denied any help, because they were regarded by the factor of the day as uncooperative. Their desperation led to an unwilling attempt – Inuit are extremely law-abiding – to raid the Hudson's Bay Company store at night. When the raiders were caught, the people say one of them was beaten so badly by the factor that he subsequently died, and that the following day the goods the raiders had attempted to steal were dumped in the sea to demonstrate that the local whites would rather destroy food than allow Inuit to have it on credit.

The fur trade was built upon the economics of dependency. From the hunters' point of view, this was grounded in certain extremely valuable trade goods – notably ever improving rifles and ammunition. It was augmented by forms of addiction – to tea, tobacco, sugar and, in some Subarctic regions, alcohol. Over time, the exchange at the trading post became habitual, and a

*

When non-Dene came to our land,
we saw them as curious strangers who had come
to visit; we shared with them and helped them to survive.
We could not conceive that they would not see the world as we do.
We trusted what people said, for that was the way we had lived
amongst ourselves. The Dene had no experience or
understanding of a people who would
try to control us, or who would
say that somehow they owned
the land we had always
lived on.

Stephen Kakfwi
Fort Good Hope

*

new set of seasonal movements and technologies evolved. There thus arose a culture of the fur trade, with its own traditions and skills. Preparation of furs, negotiating their price, knowing where fine fur species would be found in different years and at different seasons – these all supplemented older practice and knowledge. As a result of the fur trade, whites established themselves as a powerful force in every part of the Arctic and Subarctic. In some regions, because of the Hudson's Bay Company's charter and its right – indeed, obligation – to administer the vast territory of what was called Rupert's Land, traders not only controlled the supply of ever more important goods, but also were able to act as lawmaker, law enforcer, judge and jury. The economic relationship between fur trader and northern peoples was underpinned by the beginnings of the political relationships that have shaped frontiers in northern Canada ever since.

In becoming trappers, most hunters changed their economic lives to benefit from trade with white newcomers. The hunting and trapping mix is among the first and most important example of the hunters' wish to accommodate and benefit from innovation. And this accommodation meant that the economy of the north as a whole was based on the knowledge and skills of aboriginal peoples. Without their co-operation, the early days of Canadian economic development would have been impossible. Despite the dependency that fur traders had to establish among hunters to advance their purpose, the place of trappers in the economy as a whole gave them a real importance and a certain dignity.

In the 1920s and 1930s, in part as a result of the Depression striking North American urban and agricultural life, large numbers of whites moved northward to become trappers. Fur prices during the period remained surprisingly strong. This influx of white trappers precipitated an era of conflict and confusion throughout much of the Subarctic. At the same time, provincial governments wished to establish that they – and not the Can-

adian federal government – had responsibility for wildlife and its harvesting stock. This combination of circumstances led to the trapline registration programme, begun in 1926, according to which all trapping was to be licensed and administered by provincial authorities. The original idea was that a trapper would be granted a licence to set a line of traps, and that this line would be marked on maps prepared by provincial wildlife offices. This plan gave rise to the term 'trapline', although very soon it was replaced by a scheme that designated trapping areas. Many hunting and trapping families were persuaded to register their areas under the provincial scheme; they were told that if they did not do so they would lose all rights in their land and be vulnerable to displacement by white competitors.

In northern British Columbia, Alberta and Saskatchewan, the registration programme worked very much to the advantage of provincial authority and white newcomers. Further north, beyond the reach of roads, registration programmes were set up, but these made little difference to the peoples' way of using their land. It is ironic that the one attempt to administer northern peoples' economic life was accompanied by, if not aimed at, a reduction of their right to live it. Throughout the 1930s and 1940s, however, trapping continued to be a mainstay of most northern families. Fur prices continued high, despite fluctuations, until 1947. Since then, prices collapsed, remained low throughout the 1950s and 1960s, then rallied. Some groups continued to trap as they always had. Others adjusted their life away from trapping and towards a more complete reliance on hunting. Others were affected – as we shall see – by other frontier activities. For all the northern peoples, however, the right to trap in the ways and places they regard as their own is upheld in defiance of all opposing forces.

Trapping has had consequences for every aspect of northern culture. The patterns of authority, seasonal movement, inter-

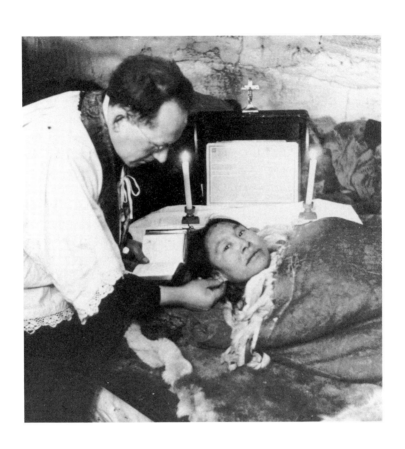

group exchange, choice of clothing and even language all reveal the influence of the trapping life. But the foundation of the cultures has continued to be hunting. The structure of the seasonal round comes from the demands of a hunting system; trapping has caused adjustments, some temporary and others permanent, but no fundamental revision of the system. Similarly, the nature of respect, sharing and spirituality are all rooted in the hunting way of life. Trapping has drawn on these to its advantage; it is no coincidence that so many hunters became excellent trappers.

Whaling and the fur trade opened the door to the advance of the frontiers of Christianity. The people of the far north constituted a human and moral resource for European and North American missionaries. Taking advantage of its routes and new infrastructures, missionaries followed (and sometimes pushed beyond) the whaling and fur trade posts. In relying upon and collaborating with traders, missionaries also tended to underpin the moral superiority and reinforce the economic purposes of newcomers. Catholics and Protestants vied with one another for control of regions, villages and even individuals. After much indecent haste and intra-religious factionalism, the two large Christian systems shared most of the northern territory between themselves. On the basis of Christian appearances – attendance at church and official membership of a denomination – the religious frontier had spread across the north by 1940. In more recent times, various sects and denominations have challenged the main Christian religions, and have continued the eager quest for northern converts.

By and large, Christianity has achieved a widespread but superficial success throughout the far north. Virtually all northern hunting families have allied themselves to one or another version of the Christian message, and go through the motions of the appropriate rites of passage and seasonal rituals. This missionary success has been helped by hunters' adaptability and flexibility: their shamanistic spiritual system does not, intrinsi-

cally, exclude the possibility of Christian ideas. Indeed, several Dene groups, having heard about Christianity before they encountered Christian missionaries in person, quickly developed forms of syncretism – they incorporated parts of Christian theology into their own spiritualism. Some Dene shamans made spirit journeys to heaven, where they met God or Jesus and received detailed information about the coming of the white man, seventh day observance, Christian marriage rules and – in several striking cases – the end of the world by explosion and fire.

Missionaries took advantage of shamanistic openness to new ideas, and insinuated their doctrines into existing belief systems. Then, once basic ideas were accepted and alongside increasing dependence on white services and trade, missionaries used their growing influence and power to suppress the shamanism by which their early approaches had been so helped. Many missionaries, assisted by having learned the hunters' languages, told people that what they believed was true, but that the spirits central to shamanism constituted the devils in Christian theology. Paradoxically this encouraged some of the profound and lasting integration of Christian ideas into existing spiritual systems. At the same time, missionaries could point out that the peoples' own shamans were unable to cure new diseases – measles, tuberculosis and influenza – which were sweeping the Arctic and, in many areas, causing terrible population losses. In the single year 1928, one sixth of the entire Dene population died in a flu epidemic. The Christian message could all too easily appear to explain why hunters were vulnerable to these diseases, but whites were immune: the non-believer would die. At the same time, Christian death encompassed its own remedy: believers would have eternal life.

As a result of Christianity, shamanism among the Inuit is extremely hard to discern. Spirit possession, journeys to consult dominant spiritual forces, use of the drum to contact, summon or express spirit power, diagnosis and cure of illness by understand-

ing and removal of alien spiritual influences – these and similar practices are very rare or well concealed. To some extent, fundamentalist and Low Church rituals have provided ways in which shamanistic approaches to religion can be expressed. Speaking in tongues, the power of faith that allows you, for example, to walk on water, and even sheer intensity of belief – these are aspects of some forms of Christianity that accord with aboriginal ideas and psychology. But the fullness and freedom of shamanism have been stifled in the far north. Clear religious and spiritual dependence is no longer upon men and women who are able to make contact with the spirit world of the air, sea and land. Instead, religious experience is hard to dissociate from dependence upon, and to some extent a subservience to, the advocates of Christian belief.

Among the Dene, where Catholicism has been more generally successful in the competition for new souls than Protestant rivals, shamanistic spiritual beliefs and practices are surprisingly strong. Dreaming, individual spirit quests and widespread acceptance of a spiritualized nature of the environment all play a part in many Dene communities. To some extent, syncretism has facilitated a coexistence between shamanism and Christianity: in the nineteenth century, some influential Athapaskan shamans had visions of the Christian moral and material cosmos, and managed to establish their own shamanistic interpretation of what was to come. In this way, God and Jesus were given places in creation stories, taboo observance rules and the dream experience. Syncretism of this kind also occurred, and continues to play a part, in the spiritual lives of Cree and Naskapi. In all cases, however, the spread of Christianity has been inseparable from a systematic and effective campaign by missionaries and their zealous converts to undermine shamanistic ideas and influences. In this way, for most northern hunting peoples, the elaborate spiritual dimensions of their environment have been supplemented and sometimes undermined by a relatively

simplistic Christian world view.

The Christian frontier was not the only ideological or moral venture among the hunting peoples of the north. The region also constituted a national frontier: an edge of Canada that was little known and of uncertain sovereignty. In the late nineteenth and twentieth centuries, ownership of offshore islands and water-ways became a matter of anxious international debate. At the same time, Canada as a country looked to its northern edges for future economic strength: the national economy had always rested on frontier resource extraction. The disorders of the gold rush made Yukon Territory famous – and also brought the Royal Northwest Mounted Police into the Subarctic in the 1890s. Similarly, police followed the whalers to the Arctic Ocean in 1895. And to establish Canada's claim to all High Arctic islands and waterways and to set in place the possibility of future resource frontiers, after 1920 Royal Canadian Mounted Police (RCMP) detachments were set up in a network of outposts through the Subarctic and Arctic frontiers.

In the early days, these policemen had the job of flying the flag, exploring the terrain and ministering to the native peoples. They took over payment of welfare from the Hudson's Bay Com-pany factors, distributed relief in cases of emergency, and had the job of labelling, numbering and recording all Inuit and Dene individuals. Here was the beginning of Canadian adminis-tration, the extension of the government frontier itself.

The RCMP also enforced Canadian law in dramatic and sym-bolic fashion. In particular, the Inuit practice of assisting people who had decided to commit suicide was interpreted by Canadian law enforcers as murder. In cases that achieved national notor-iety, hunters were charged and tried for doing what their culture required of them. Also, Inuit who killed in self-defence or to remove the threat of a dangerous deviant found themselves charged with murder and sent to southern prisons. These were dramatic instances of a new authority seeking to establish its

211

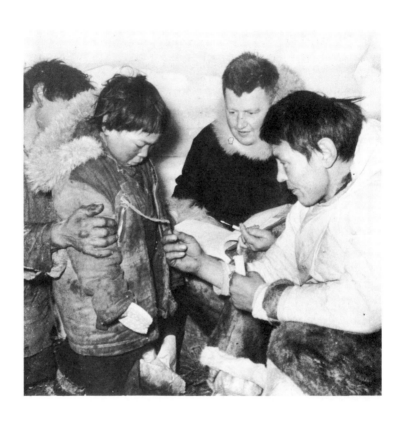

rules and showing its extraordinary power. It also fell to the RCMP to explain and enforce southern rules and laws. Everywhere this was backed by inducements and force: officers handed out welfare and wore side-arms. Through the early work of the RCMP in the north, the hunting peoples were shown that the white man could dispense both largesse and a startlingly sharp form of justice. The police consolidated what traders and missionaries had begun: between the three agencies, the newcomers claimed the right to determine the bases of economic, moral and social life. Dependence was compounded by institutional subordinacy.

By the 1950s the sequence of frontiers had brought certain advantages, complicated changes and a crisis to the hunters of the Arctic and Subarctic regions. Every aspect of life was affected. Dependence upon the fur trade meant vulnerability to fur prices. Store bought clothing and prefabricated houses were supposed to be better or more sophisticated than caribou suits and trapping cabins. Candy, pop and cheap groceries were supplanting or displacing the pure meat and fat diet. Christianity was being urged as truer and better than shamanism. Children had been taken away from homes in accord with southern educational ideals. Wage employment was upheld as the only economic hope for the future. Perhaps most important of all, the spread of white frontiersmen in the north had led to terrible outbursts of viral and bacterial infections. Each summer, after the ship delivered its supplies at High Arctic settlements and camps, there were deaths as a result of new strains of influenza, measles and similar illnesses. Throughout the north, tuberculosis was out of control. In one survey, a population living in the west Hudson Bay area was discovered to have an active tuberculosis rate of over 30 per cent. From the point of view of the hunters and trappers of the north, not only their culture, but the people themselves were disappearing. What was left of their way

*

...when we first had the RCMP come around.
We were so scared of them. They were so big, they
looked like moose and musk ox to us.

Nora Ruben
Paulatuk

Our son, the son we loved best of all –
we wanted to say no, he isn't going to your school.
He was so small, so young. We wanted to refuse.
But we said yes. We were intimidated.

Simon Anaviapik
Pond Inlet

Before I went to school
the only English I knew was 'hello', and when we
got there we were told that if we spoke Indian they would
whip us until our hands were blue on both sides.
And also we were told that the Indian religion
was superstitious and pagan ... and
everyone was given a haircut
which was a bald haircut.
We all felt lost...

Dolphus Shae
Fort Franklin

The people won't take a white man's word
at face value any more because you fooled them
too many times. You took everything they had and you
gave them nothing. You took all the fur, took all the whales,
killed all the polar bear with aircraft and everything,
and put a quota on top of that, so we can't have
polar bear when we feel like it any more.
All that we pay for.

Vince Steen
Tuktoyaktuk

*

of life was undermined and devalued; the surviving people demoralized.

In 1952 and 1959 the Canadian writer Farley Mowat published two books, *People of the Deer* and *The Desperate People*, that focused attention on the plight of Canada's aboriginal peoples. Mowat's work has been viewed with some scepticism, much of its detail challenged as imaginative invention and his patronizing tone in those books cited as evidence of his irrelevance. There is no doubting, however, that Mowat was right in principle: many northern hunting groups were experiencing real hardship and, in some cases, actual starvation. All groups were living with the results of the cumulative impact of several frontiers.

At the same time, the 1950s saw a boom in large-scale industrial growth, central economic planning and social welfare planning. Inevitably, the resources of the north came under new and eager scrutiny, while its peoples seemed to be in dire need of the welfare provisions that would come only with assimilation into the mainstream of Canadian political life. In the 1950s and 1960s, much of the RCMP's work was gradually taken over by Indian Agents and other government officers. As part of the administrative endeavour, hunters and trappers were urged to live in permanent villages where social and administrative services could be effected with maximum efficiency and minimum expense. Schools and nursing stations were set up, and housing programmes provided accommodation nearby. Parents were told that they had to allow their children to be taken to white-run schools at the nearest village or regional centre. Economies of scale of administration – it is cheaper to provide services to a small number of large villages – meant that people who persisted with their seasonal rounds and flexible use of the land were an expensive problem.

Concentration of peoples in larger villages and attempts to assimilate them into an economic as well as welfare mainstream can

215

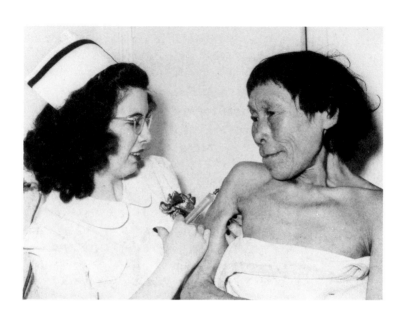

be questioned, but the provision of medical services was essential, and other help was, for the most part, well intentioned. Unfortunately, those services that the people felt they needed came in a total package including elements that appeared irrational and punitive. Many recall this as an agonizing episode in modern history, and say that they were intimidated by and dependent upon whites: when it came to schooling, they felt they had no choice but to accept a painful separation from their sons and daughters. When talking about this period in modern history, many Inuit elders use the word *ilira*, a term that means the feelings inspired by a powerful and potentially dangerous force or person that one dare not resist. Dependence upon and vulnerability to whites meant that the new administration and education policies, whatever grief they may have caused, were acquiesced in. The settlement and village era was thus a direct product of extensions of the government frontier.

Through the 1960s and 1970s, more and more northern hunting families found themselves unwillingly drawn into a web of social and economic life that paid very little heed to their long-established customs and needs. In the late 1960s, and then throughout the 1970s, elders and spokespersons among northern peoples began to protest against the evident decline in cultural wellbeing. An upsurge in worldwide demands by oppressed societies gave northern hunters both the idiom and the confidence to make their own protest at the course of events. At the same time parents were alarmed and frightened by the wide gulf opening between them and their children, and the very existence of their cultures thus being placed in jeopardy. Their protest went alongside a passionate revival and restatement of cultural beliefs and economic activities. The people conducted their own studies into their systems of land use and resource management, and discovered that these – along with their own established wisdom – demonstrated the extent to which their ways of understanding and using their lands had persisted despite the cumu-

lative impact of frontiers. Restatement of aboriginal right in the north, therefore, came in part as a reaction to the 1950s.

In the 1970s and 1980s, the hydrocarbon industry has spawned a new northern frontier. Since the discovery of rich oil and natural gas deposits in northern Alaska in 1968, geological attention and pipeline construction interests have focused with great eagerness on High Arctic islands and the Beaufort Sea. They have not been disappointed. Oil and gas fields have been located, airstrips and access roads have been built, more frontiersmen have arrived from the south and some production is underway in the western Subarctic and Arctic. There is eruptively optimistic talk of energy corridors that may follow the Mackenzie Valley from the Beaufort Sea and on to the United States–Canadian border, as well as a delivery system that would cut across the eastern barren lands, linking the High Arctic with midwestern and eastern cities. Meanwhile, advocates of shipping on the high seas dream of massive ice-breaking tankers carrying liquid natural gas from as far north as Ellesmere Island down the eastern seaboard of North America.

The oil and gas frontier has raised the question of employment opportunities and economic assimilation in a new and clear form. Its proponents argue that here lies an opportunity for northern hunters and trappers to benefit in a very direct way from economic development of their territories: they say that jobs will be available and opportunities for entrepreneurial development in secondary sectors will proliferate as a result of oil and gas exploration and subsequent extraction. These advocates of the new opportunities point to places like Tuktoyaktuk on the High Arctic coastline and Norman Wells in the upper Mackenzie Valley, saying that here are places where northern peoples have taken good advantage of a new kind of economic prosperity.

In fact, many had already taken advantage of wage employment opportunities that came with earlier frontier activities. Men and women worked for the whalers in the nineteenth cen-

tury, and provided services on a regular, paid basis to fur traders. Missionaries, in some cases, employed guides and cleaning women. The growth of the new settlements in the 1950s and 1960s generated construction, maintenance and other kinds of jobs. For the most part, hunting peoples' flexibility extends to an enthusiastic readiness to incorporate every sort of opportunity into their system. Hunters' involvement and dependence upon the fur trade, followed by their movement to regular residency at an administrative centre, have meant that hunting itself has required equipment and fuels that can be acquired only with cash. Hunters and trappers have come to need money to hunt and trap. Some can get enough money through the fur trade but, as we have seen, this has proved an uncertain source of income – especially in the light of intense international pressure on fur prices. Some finance hunting by carving for the art trade or selling narwhal and walrus ivory. In the Subarctic sale of moccasins, jackets and beadwork ensures a cash income. All these extensions of subsistence into trade gain relatively small returns when compared with a job at a settlement or in one or another frontier sector. This need for money, to buy guns, skidoos and groceries, reinforces hunters' flexibility: if periodic wage labour can ensure that they, or some other member of their household, can hunt and trap with maximum effectiveness, then a wage labour job is part of what is wanted and needed.

What northern hunters and trappers have never accepted, however, is that destruction of *their* lands, or *their* form of economic life, could be a price worth paying for what the newcomers had to offer. If whalers had told the people that one result of this new activity would be the virtual annihilation of bowhead whales and walruses throughout the far north, no doubt Inuit hunters would have refused to co-operate and would have demanded that the whalers cease their activities and go home. The hunters do not reject innovation; but they have made it clear that, above all else, they value the integrity of their lands and the

continuing possibility for making their kind of use of their own resources.

Not surprisingly, therefore, Inuit, Dene, Cree, Naskapi, Innu and Métis have all opposed the new development frontier. Some, of course, have taken jobs with oil and gas companies and at mines. But limited expansion or modernization of the hunting and trapping economy has meant an imbalance of employment opportunities. Investment in wage-labour sectors is not matched by development or protection of hunting and trapping. While the drastic fall in sealskin prices in the 1980s has underlined the cash-dependency even of the most determined hunting families.

All the people fear for their land and for their cultural survival: the possibility of hunting and trapping requires a constant check on frontier activities that impede the possible coexistence of different kinds of northern economic life. Just as the gold rush provided a reason for signing Treaties 8 and 11 with the Dene, so the latest frontier flurry has played an important part in effecting negotiations and even settlements between the Canadian government and the people of northern Quebec (in relation to the James Bay hydroelectric venture) and the Inuvialuit of the Mackenzie Delta (in relation to the Beaufort Sea oil exploration and development). The purpose of these new negotiations and settlements, like the real intention behind the treaties in the nineteenth and early twentieth centuries, is to guarantee that northern hunters will be able to choose the way of life they wish to follow. They will have no choice, they point out, if their territories and cultures are destroyed by the frontiers of the south.

Chapter 12

The Politics of Survival

Cree and Dene will say that a person seized with anger, eaten with impatience, is a victim of an enemy's medicine. Inuit regard anger as childish and self-defeating, a sign that a person's *isuma* has failed to develop. Dene view impatience as a danger. Gentleness, hospitality and patience are essential to hunting life, inseparable from its demands, integral to its cultures.

The aboriginal cultures of the north find themselves in the economic and political hinterlands of other people's nation states – including the USSR and USA as well as Canada. Much has been done by these countries that sits uneasily with northern peoples' ways of thinking and acting in the world. To be a part of someone else's frontier is to be exposed to many political and social dangers. Compromise with newcomers may be possible, at times even beneficial. But when the distant centre claims the very land on which hunters and trappers live, hospitality must discover its limits. When newcomers ignore requests that hunters' and trappers' rights be respected and their system of law be followed, patience becomes inappropriate. When cultural and material loss put survival itself at stake, gentleness achieves very little.

Seen through the eyes of northern elders, modern politics may appear shrill and distasteful. And there may be a real possibility that the methods demanded by political campaigning and activism undermine the very cultures that such campaigns seek to defend. But these are risks of which the people are well aware. They have chosen to use the white man's ways to defend their lands and rights. This may be difficult and distasteful, but it is the politics of survival.

Northern hunting societies' ways of life exist *with* the land. Health is based on connections between social and natural systems, between forms of authority, mobility, child-raising or

language and meat, fish, trees, ice or the land itself. Such connections are not quaint or romantic; from them come individual strength, family happiness and the very tissue of culture; and upon them depends the future. When the connections are broken, modern ills begin. To resist these ills, and to repair the damage already caused by frontiers, has required modern politics. Yet the nature of the connections that these politics must seek to maintain or repair raises questions of authority and jurisdiction, questions about who will decide the shapes of social life and organization, as well as – perhaps because of – questions of ecology and environmental economics.

Negotiations aimed at answering these political questions create a sharp encounter of ideological and moral opposites. Northern aboriginal peoples are egalitarian; those with whom they negotiate seek hierarchical solutions to all problems. Hunters and trappers maintain subtle, sensitive and complex approaches to the world in order to keep it in its present or natural balance; representatives of modern nation states – developers, civil servants, frontiersmen – express an energetic belief in future wealth in stark, simple terms. For the peoples of the north, social and environmental protection depend on their communities having real power over their lands. For officials in capital cities, power must always reside at the centre – if not of their own nation, then in one of its provinces.

Egalitarianism is opposed to hierarchy, subtlety to simplification, community to centralized power. And beyond these oppositions is a different kind of belief in the future. Hunters do not trust their power to shape new kinds of future; they seek to meet an unpredictable world with a careful consolidation of powers, beliefs and customs in which they have trusted for hundreds, even thousands of years. Here is a profound, and profoundly true, conservatism.

Industrial and industrializing nation states espouse the most sanguine confidence in the future, confident – albeit blindly – in

being able to solve whatever problems and overcome whatever damage their economic development might cause. Here is the perpetual radicalism of the ideology of growth.

Hunters say: we must be sure that we shall not owe our grand-children an apology. Northern developers, living in a simplified ideological universe, have no such fears.

The originality and problem of northern politics is clear. A system of authority that is based upon the inseparability of land, animals and a society that seeks to ensure the renewability of its resources challenges some of the working assumptions of modern political life. The dominating nation states of the north are com-mitted to a form of economic growth that assumes that con-stantly growing needs will be met by new, though often unknown, resources. Aboriginal peoples' prosperity does not rely on any such belief in future resources nor on the generation of new needs. For them, therefore, participation in government that develops the land on a non-renewable basis cannot be a solution. Assimilation into institutions of power that set profit above place and sacrifice the future to the present represents a loss of power.

Since the 1960s, northern hunting peoples have negotiated a series of policies and agreements with central governments. These were made against a background of drastic threats to their lands and ways of life. The discovery of oil on the Alaskan north slope and rumours of nuclear blasts being used to create a deep-water harbour in south-east Alaska helped give rise to an Alas-kan native rights movement, which shaped the Alaska Land Claims Act of 1971. This activity in the United States prompted similar Canadian movements. In 1969, partly in reaction to oil and gas exploration and development in the Mackenzie Delta, the Inuvialuit of that area established the Committee of Original People's Entitlement (COPE). Two years later, a Canadian national Inuit organization, Inuit Tapirisat of Canada (ITC),

*

The other day I was taking a walk
in Yellowknife . . . and I passed a house there with
a dog tied outside. I didn't notice it and all of a sudden
this dog jumped up and gave me a big bark,
and then, after I passed through there, I was saying to myself,
'Well, that dog taught me a lesson.' You know, so often you see
the native people, they are tied down too much, I think,
by the government. We never go and bark,
therefore nobody takes notice of us,
and it is about time that we
the people of this northland should
get up sometime and bark.

Jim Sittichinli
Aklavik

We want to govern our own lives
and our own lands and its resources. We want
to have our own system of government, by which we can
control and develop our land for our benefit.
We want to have the exclusive right to hunt, to fish
and to trap . . . We must again become a people making
our own history. To be able to make our own
history is to be able to mould our own future,
to build our society that preserves the
best of our past and our traditions, while
enabling us to grow and develop
as a whole people.

Robert Andre
Arctic Red River

Does the federal government not consider us to be human
too? Do they think we don't make history?

Richard Nerysoo
Fort McPherson

*

literally 'the people's team' or 'collaboration', and often translated as Eskimo Brotherhood, was formed in Ottawa. This has
been followed by the emergence of the Indian Brotherhood,
representing the Dene of the Northwest Territories, the Council
of Yukon Indians, the Grand Council of Chiefs among the James
Bay Cree, the Labrador Inuit Association, several Métis associ-
ations, organizations among the Naskapi and Montagnais in
Quebec, the Kaska-Dena in northern British Columbia, as well
as new groupings based on peoples whose lands were covered by
old treaties of dubious legality.

The momentum that gave birth to these and other political
groups continued to build through the 1970s and 1980s. It was
helped by Pierre Trudeau's 1969 policy paper declaring that the
Canadian government intended to abolish special status for
Indian people and effectively denying the whole idea of aboriginal right. Angry reaction caused Canadian governments to
reconsider, and finally to agree – under some pressure from the
1971 Supreme Court ruling on the Nishga case – that aboriginal
right did exist, and would have to be defined.

From 1971 to 1973, the James Bay Cree and Inuit of Arctic
Quebec struggled to prevent the damming of all major rivers in
the north-west corner of Quebec and the flooding of hundreds of
square miles of Cree and Inuit lands. They failed to stop the project, but achieved a compensatory settlement that recognized
their title to 5,200 square miles of hunting lands, exclusive hunting, fishing and trapping rights on another 60,000 square miles,
and a set of benefits that included extensive support for families
that chose to live on and from the land.

But the James Bay agreement, along with other groups' negotiating positions, was criticized for failing to insist on entrenchment of aboriginal right and the establishment of a jursidiction
or system of authority that would guarantee northern peoples'
unchallengeable control of their territories. The critics felt that
the oppositions between aboriginal and Euro-Canadian world

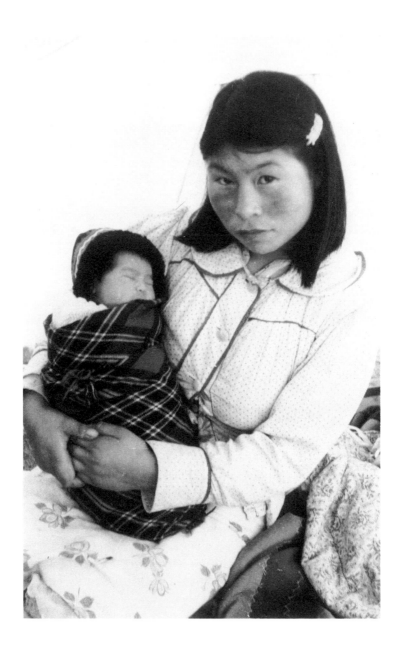

views and culture were being resolved in favour of Quebec City and Ottawa. More and more fears were expressed that the very heart of northern aboriginal society – families who maintained and practised their own laws and customs – was being forgotten. In the case of the James Bay Cree and Quebec Inuit, this was understood at least partially as a result of duress – chiefs and elders there signed accords with a developmental gun at their heads. But in other cases, there grew an uneasy sense of compromise and possible ultimate defeat through political and developmental collaboration.

Then the Dene of the Northwest Territories emerged as a completely new kind of political force in the Canadian north. The Indian Brotherhood of the Northwest Territories made an explicit identification with struggles taking place in the Third World. Nationalism reinforced concern with cultural survival. In 1975, this was expressed in a statement known as the Dene Declaration. It began with these words:

> We the Dene of the NWT insist on the right to be regarded by ourselves and the world as a nation.
>
> And while there are realities we are forced to submit to, such as the existence of a country called Canada, we insist on the right to self-determination as a distinct people...

In 1978, the Indian Brotherhood changed its name to Dene Nation.

The impact of this approach to aboriginal rights in the Canadian north was dramatic. Other groups recognized that the Dene had now expressed a real aspiration – for equality and independence, for the political space within which to continue to grow as distinct societies based on renewable resources. The nationalist expression of the issue created a sense of possible jurisdictional fences around northern cultures, an image of real guarantees for the people's chosen ways of using their resources and for the land

*

Development has to be something
that is transferring control to the people ... What
we are saying is that development should be
orderly, it should be planned, it should be at the
pace of the local people, it should benefit
local people.

Georges Erasmus
Yellowknife

... my belief is that if we all stand up together and
fight for what we want, and not give up, we might
accomplish something for ourselves and for the
future of our children.

Charlie Snowshoe
Mackenzie Valley

When an Indian breathes, it's politics.

Cindy Gilday
Yellowknife

*

itself. Here, it seemed, was the expression of a new political order in the north. The encounter between the opposite ideologies, between hunters' world views and Canadian ideas about the north, looked as though it might be resolved in favour of hunters and trappers.

The terms of the debate about lands and cultures were changed, but there was a new polarization. The Dene approach to the issue was as alarming to the average Canadian as it was coherent to northern hunters. Dene leaders were looking for profound changes. They also insisted that negotiating sessions with government officials include a group of Dene elders, whose understanding of the issues and acceptance of any proposals be secured there and then. The Dene Nation was attacked fiercely for being obstructive as well as revolutionary.

Throughout Canada the argument continues – and may well continue for another generation. Indeed, this is not an issue to which there is some final solution. Negotiation of aboriginal rights can   and perhaps should – be a permanent feature on the political map. But there have been milestones along the way. At the hearings held by the Berger Inquiry into the Mackenzie Valley pipeline proposal in the late 1970s, the peoples' consistent, eloquent and impassioned demand that their lands and lives be respected and left in the charge of the societies that have lived there for thousands of years reached the ears, and even the hearts, of millions of North Americans. Debate in the 1980s about the division of the Northwest Territories into two new jurisdictions, Nunavut and Denendeh, the one Inuit, the other Dene, has brought at least some recognition of the peoples' wish for power over their own lives and lands. Court decisions confirming James Bay Cree aboriginal right *despite* the James Bay agreement, the Innu demand for Ntesinan, their own jurisdiction in the Labrador–Quebec Peninsula, and the continuing arguments for proper recognition of the spirit of the treaties with Dene groups in British Columbia, Alberta and Saskatchewan –

these all express needs and fears that hunters have felt since whites first called northern homelands the south's frontier.

Division of the Northwest Territories and creation of new political institutions do not, of themselves, ensure the peoples' authority and jurisdiction. Whether or not the changes will achieve what old treaties and new settlements so far have failed to achieve – entrenchment rather than loss of aboriginal authority – depends on the details of new forms of northern government. A central difficulty lies in how white newcomers' interests should and should not be protected. There are awkward questions about the status of new authorities within Canadian Confederation and about how aboriginal peoples can protect their rights against potential floods of southern immigrants. In areas with histories marked and marred by boom and bust economics, from the gold rush in the Yukon to hydrocarbon exploration throughout the north to NATO bases in Labrador, indigenous groups are aware of how quickly, if temporarily, they can be overwhelmed by sheer numbers.

Proposals for dealing with this kind of difficulty have ranged from suggestions that northern white towns be made into reserves for newcomers, to a residency requirement of between three and five years for voting, to division of new governments in a way that will ensure aboriginal communities have a veto on all policies affecting their people. At the same time, those northern hunters and trappers who live in provinces rather than the Northwest Territories or the Yukon have to find ways of overcoming provincial claims that all lands outside reserves belong to the Crown, i.e. the Province, and not to the people who have lived there for thousands of years. While newcomers to the Territories or settlers and frontiersmen in the provinces feel free to take, use and, in many areas, devastate the land, the peoples' demands for new jurisdictional arrangements will continue to be central to their future wellbeing.

Behind the specifics of all the proposals to protect aboriginal culture and land are the concerns that have been the subject of this book. The demands are for recognition, the discarding of absurd and self-serving stereotypes; the right to continue to live as equal, modern peoples; a chance to live their own egalitarian individualism, and to raise their children according to their own ideals of human and natural life. As we learn about these demands, and about the cultural forms upon which they are based, we see across a considerable distance; there is no short cut from urban industrial consciousness, with its brief history and roots in European peasant life, to the cultures of the north that have evolved over millennia a precise, yet flexible place in an environment so different from our own. We may discover that aboriginal peoples have customs and beliefs with strengths and truth that we wish to adopt. There is much in the far north from which those in the temperate south can learn. The distances between south and north, peasant and hunter, city and bush are nonetheless vast.

Resonances of the politics of northern peoples' survival are also great: the wish for a political control that resides in the hands of those who know and use the world's resources; the longing for a greater equality; the need for decentralization; the wish to protect the land for our grandchildren; the conservatism that espouses, with real radicalism, the notion that needs and wealth should not be expanded as if the world's resources were limitless; a longing to raise children in ways that generate less anxiety; a desire to speak one's own language, be it of another place or another class, without fear or shame; and the wish for an individualism that is not bound up with hierarchy and privilege.

The politics pursued by aboriginal peoples are not of isolated, limited interest. The native rights movement in Canada implicates everyone. Its details may seem parochial; its implications could hardly be greater.

241

Photograph Captions and Credits

In the case of archival photographs, captions and credits are based on such information as is available. Sometimes this is scant. *N.p.* means that no photographer has been identified; *n.d.* that the date a picture was taken is unknown. The number preceding each caption is the page on which the photograph can be found.

Monochrome plates

vi. *Frontispiece.* Ida Aivek, Holman Island, wearing parka with wolverine hood, characteristic of western Arctic. *Ulli Steltzer, 1980.*

1. English explorers in a skirmish with Inuit. Copy after a lost John White original, perhaps showing a scene on Baffin Island during Frobisher's second voyage, 1577. *Trustees of the British Museum, Department of Prints and Drawings.*

2. Mountains in winter, North Baffin Island. *Ulli Steltzer, 1980.*

4. Probably Cree, photo identified only as 'making birch syrup, 1900–1930'. *n.p. Public Archives of Canada*

6. Kanadise Uyarashuk and Charlene, in their home in Igloolik in the eastern Arctic. *J. C. H. King, 1986.*

8. Dene fisherman, Whitestone River, Northwest Territories. *J. L. Grew, c 1945. Public Archives of Canada.*

10. Fishermen on sea ice loading arctic char into sack, Paulatuk. *Ulli Steltzer, 1980.*

12. The House family at their hunting camp, north of La Grande River, Quebec. *J. C. H. King, 1986.*

14. Sea ice near Igloolik. *Ulli Steltzer, 1980.*

16. Hudson's Bay Company ships *Prince of Wales* and *Eddystone* bartering with Inuit of the Upper Savage Islands, Hudson Strait. *Watercolour by Robert Hood (1797–1821), 1819. Public Archives of Canada.*

18. (above) Naskapi hunters and caribou. Watercolour by William Hind (1833–88), 1861. Hind and his brother Henry made the first European expedition to the interior of the Labrador peninsula. *Notman Archives, McCord Museum, McGill University, Montreal.*

18. (below) Labrador hunter in kayak. Marked 'drawn from nature', by Peter Rindisbacker, 1821. *Public Archives of Canada.*

20. Marked: 'Nanook enjoying a Harry Lauder record'. This is a still from Flaherty's film *Nanook of the North* or a location picture by Flaherty. *From the Coward Album, Notman Archives, McCord Museum, McGill University, Montreal.*

23. Cree at summer gathering, Great Whale River, Quebec. *S. J.*

243

Bailey, *Department of Indian and Northern Affairs, 1948. Public Archives of Canada.*

35. Padleimiut woman scraping frost from the ice window inside a snow house, west Hudson Bay. *Richard Harrington, c 1950. Public Archives of Canada.*

36. A Naskapi group at their winter camp. The man's name is given as Steamash. *n.p., n.d. National Museums of Canada, Ottawa.*

40. Copper Inuit woman at caribou-skin tent, Dolphin and Union Straits, central Arctic. *Diamond Jenness, 1916. National Museums of Canada, Ottawa.*

42. Igloolik hunters at the ice edge. Small boats are used for retrieving seals when they have been shot. *Ulli Steltzer, 1980.*

44. Eskimo Point village during spring thaw. *Ulli Steltzer, 1981.*

46. Woman fishing through an ice hole, George River, Quebec. *Ulli Steltzer, 1981.*

48. Repulse Bay family on a skidoo, crossing sea ice. *Ulli Steltzer, 1981.*

51. Butchering a beluga at Little Whale River, Quebec. *n.p., c 1880. Notman Archives, McCord Museum, McGill University, Montreal.*

52. A woman eating with her ulu, the half-moon-shaped knife used by women throughout the Arctic. The metal headband suggests this was taken in west Hudson Bay Barren Lands. *n.p., c 1950. Anglican Archives, Toronto.*

54. Ojibwa preparing dry meat. Marked 'Singeing moose head for food'. *F. W. Waugh, 1916. National Museums of Canada, Ottawa.*

56. Dry meat at Baker Lake. *Ulli Steltzer, 1981.**

58. Dogrib man pulling lake trout, Great Bear Lake, Northwest Territories. *C. B. Osgood, 1928–9. National Museums of Canada, Ottawa.*

60. Columban Pujardjuk eating char. Pelly Bay, central Arctic. *Ulli Steltzer, 1980.*

64. Community banquet, Grise Fjord. *Ulli Steltzer, 1980.**

66. Arctic char cache among the rocks, eastern Arctic. *Ulli Steltzer, 1980.*

69. Natalino Attagutaluk skinning a caribou, Igloolik. *Ulli Steltzer, 1980.*

72. Hunter pulling in two ringed seals, Igloolik. *Richard Harrington, 1952. Public Archives of Canada.*

74. Dene setting traps, northern Manitoba. *Richard Harrington, 1950. Hudson's Bay Company.*

76. Dene woman stretching beaver skin. *Richard Harrington, 1949. Hudson's Bay Company.*

80. Scraping skin of an arctic loon (great northern diver), Lake Harbour. *Nelson H. H. Graburn, 1960.*

82. Window display of polar bear skins at Harvey Nichols, Knightsbridge, London. *n.p., 1929. Hudson's Bay Company.*

84. Martha Kigoktak using ulu to scrape fat off polar bear skin, Grise Fjord. *Ulli Steltzer, 1980.*
87. Hunter beside a kayak, upturned umiak (larger boat) and two sealskin tents on beach, Peel River, Northwest Territories. *C. W. Mathers, 1901. Public Archives of Canada.*
90. Dene at spring camp, smoking fish, Great Bear Lake, Northwest Territories. *C. B. Osgood, 1928–9. National Museums of Canada, Ottawa.*
92. Family returning from camp to Nain, Labrador. *Ulli Steltzer, 1981.*
94. Inuit portaging kayak among remains of pressure ice on beach. *n.p., dated 1902–27. Notman Archives, McCord Museum, McGill University, Montreal.*
96. Cree tents at summer camp, Quebec. *Edmund James Peck, n.d. Anglican Archives, Toronto.*
98. Square dance at Baker Lake. *Ulli Steltzer, 1981.*
102. Loaded double sledge and dog, central Arctic. *Diamond Jenness(?), c 1915. National Museums of Canada, Ottawa.*
106. Natalino Attagutaluk, Igloolik. *Ulli Steltzer, 1980.*
108. Pelly Bay settlement. *Ulli Steltzer, 1980.*
111. Annmor uma drumming at autumn camp, central Arctic. *Diamond Jenness(?), c 1915. National Museums of Canada.*
114. Natalino Attagutaluk drumming. Igloolik. *Ulli Steltzer, 1979.**
116. Spring camp of the House family, near the mouth of La Grande River, Quebec. *J. C. H. King, 1986.*
120. Christopher Attagutaluk and ringed seal, Igloolik. *Ulli Steltzer, 1980.**
122. Copper Inuit drum dance in large snow house. The house has been cut away for photography. *R. S. Finnie, Department of Indian and Northern Affairs, 1931. Public Archives of Canada.*
126. Group at trial of Sinissiak and Uluksak, two Copper Inuit charged with murdering a Catholic priest. On Sinissiak's left is Koeha, witness for the prosecution. On Uluksak's right is Patsy Klenkerberg, interpreter. Behind stand the lawyers for the defence and the Crown. *Taken in Edmonton, Alberta, 1917. Glenbow Museum, Calgary.*
128. Moravian mission in Labrador. *Watercolour by Midshipman(?) Hall, c 1800–30. Public Archives of Canada.*
130. Maxim Marion, Métis guide. *n.p., 1872. Public Archives of Canada.*
132. Moravian Church Service, Nain, Labrador. *Ulli Steltzer, 1981.*
135. Peter Morgan and his son Matthew, George River, Quebec. *Ulli Steltzer, 1981.**
138. Dene woman with child in a moss bag, Fort Resolution, Northwest Territories. *n.p., marked '1905–31'. Public Archives of Canada.*
140. Child and sealskins, Holman Island. *Ulli Steltzer, 1980.**
142. Padleimiut woman visited by Harrington during the 1949–50 star-

vation among Inuit of the Barren Lands, west Hudson Bay. *Richard Harrington, 1950. Public Archives of Canada.*

144. Roman Catholic school, Fort Resolution. *n.p., n.d. Vale Photos, Anglican Archives, Toronto.*

146. Paulatuk children in summer. *Ulli Steltzer, 1980.*

149. Notice at Igloolik in syllabics (the writing system devised by missionaries for northern Indians and adapted for Inuktitut in the 1880s) and English. *Ulli Steltzer, 1980.*

152. Children playing on shore ice in August, Holman Island. *Ulli Steltzer, 1980.*

154. Man with arctic loon (black-throated diver), eastern Arctic. *J. C. H. King, 1986.*

156. Dance in summer, in school building, eastern Arctic. *Nelson H. H. Graburn, 1960.*

160. Page from eastern Arctic Revivalist hymnal published by the Christian Arctic Fellowship, Baker Lake, Northwest Territories. The syllabics in the life-saver ring translate as 'God's words'. *n.p., 1987. British Museum.*

162. Page from Dogrib language book used at Rae Edzo, Northwest Territories, for teaching Dene children to read and write. *n.p., 1982. Government of the Northwest Territories*

164. Elijah Tigullaraq using computer, Igloolik. *J. C. H. King, 1986.*

166. Children at George River, Quebec. *Ulli Steltzer, 1981.*

169. Damarris Ulayok's kitchen, Igloolik. *J. C. H. King, 1986.*

170. Dene group at Whitesand River, Northwest Territories. *J. L. Grew, Department of Indian and Northern Affairs, c 1940. Public Archives of Canada.*

172. Peter Morgan and Joshua Annanack working on snowmobile engine, George River, Quebec. *Ulli Steltzer, 1981.*

174. (above) Jacob Ipkangnak at home in prefabricated village house, Igloolik. *J. C. H. King, 1986.*

174. (below) Men at home in spring snow house lined with newspaper for insulation and to minimize dripping, Igloolik. *Richard Harrington, 1953. Public Archives of Canada.*

176. Padleimiut woman doing string game, Barren Lands, Northwest Territories. *Richard Harrington, 1950. Public Archives of Canada.*

178. Igloolik carver. *Ulli Steltzer, 1980.*

182. Camp on sea ice, Eskimo Point. *Ulli Steltzer, 1981.**

184. Helen Kringorn, Pelly Bay. *Ulli Steltzer, 1980.*

187. Governor of the Hudson's Bay Company, Charles V. Sale, opening new Vancouver salesroom, Beaver House. *n.p., 1928. Hudson's Bay Company.*

188. Dene women and bagpiper, Cape Smith, Northwest Territories. *D. L. McKeard, Department of Indian and Northern Affairs, 1934. Public*

Archives of Canada.

190. Trader measuring a beaver skin at Hudson's Bay Company trading post. *n.p., 1949. Hudson's Bay Company.*

192. Inuk woman playing accordion inside a snow house, eastern Arctic. *Richard Harrington, 1952. Public Archives of Canada.*

194. Furs at Hudson's Bay Company Vancouver(?) auction house. *n.p., n.d. Hudson's Bay Company.*

196. Louis Riel, Métis leader. *n.p., c 1868, Public Archives of Canada.*

198. Dene trappers arrive at trading post, Churchill, Manitoba. *Richard Harrington, 1947. Hudson's Bay Company.*

202. Trapper with white fox furs, Sachs Harbour, western Arctic. *Ulli Steltzer, 1980.*

204. Roman Catholic priest administering last rites in a snow house near Igloolik. *Richard Harrington, c 1950. Public Archives of Canada.*

206. Cree wedding at York Factory, northern Manitoba. *R. D. Davidson, 1925. Public Archives of Canada.*

208. Prayers in school on 'Mission Day', central Arctic. *Donald Marsh, c 1950. Polar Photos.*

210. Royal Canadian Mounted Police constable, central Arctic. *n.p., n.d. Polar Photos.*

212. Police taking census and checking family allowances, Windy River, Northwest Territories. The boy is wearing a disc bearing the identification number given to all Inuit by the Canadian Fed eral Government in the 1920–70 period. *J. C. Jackson, 1950. Public Archives of Canada.*

216. Nurse injecting Inuk, Port Harrison, Quebec. *Richard Harrington, 1948. Public Archives of Canada.*

218. Modern settlement, eastern Arctic. *Ulli Steltzer, 1981.*

220. Boys loading supplies in store, Holman Island. *Ulli Steltzer, 1980.*

222. Tukilkee Kiguktak completing a small snow house of the type used for overnight camping, Grise Fjord. The last step is to cut the entrance way from inside. *Ulli Steltzer, 1980.***

225. Snowshoes and gun in tent, George River, Quebec. *Ulli Steltzer, 1981.**

226. Cree smoking a Naskapi style of pipe, Great Whale River, Quebec. *O. J. Murie, 1915. Public Archives of Canada.*

228. Negotiating the James Bay and Northern Quebec Agreement. In foreground, Chief Billy Diamond of the Grand Council of the Crees and Jean Chrétien, Minister of Indian and Northern Affairs. *P. Tailler, c 1970. Montreal Star.*

230. Group of trappers, Sachs Harbour, western Arctic. *Ulli Steltzer, 1980.**

234. Nivksinik with new-born baby that she is adopting, Sugluk, Quebec. *Nelson H. H. Graburn, 1959.*

238. Daisy Sheldon, a Teslin Dena, returning home on snowshoes after setting a fishing net under lake ice. She is carring an ice pick. Yukon Territory. *n.p., n.d. National Museums of Canada, Ottawa.*
240. Marie Debora Atsatata in her home, Nain. *Ulli Steltzer, 1981.*
242. George River boys. *Ulli Steltzer, 1981.*

* Previously published in Ulli Steltzer, *Inuit: The North in Transition*, Vancouver: Douglas and McIntyre, 1982.
** Previously published in Ulli Steltzer, *Building an Igloo*, Vancouver: Douglas and McIntyre, 1981.

Select Bibliography

The following is a list of books, articles and reports that have helped the writing of this book. The first section gives references and sources for the peoples' own voices; the second gives sources for information and opinions used for the book's twelve essays. This is not a comprehensive Arctic or Subarctic bibliography.

1. The peoples' voices

Berger, T. R., *Northern Frontier, Northern Homeland*, vol. 1, Ottawa: Minister of Supply and Services, 1977. See also transcripts of community hearings of the Mackenzie Valley Pipeline Inquiry, available at Public Archives of Canada, Ottawa, and the University Library, Cambridge, England.

Brice-Bennett, Carol (ed.), *Our Footprints Are Everywhere: Inuit Land Use and Occupancy in Labrador*, Nain, Labrador: Labrador Inuit Association, 1977.

Brody, Hugh, 'Land occupancy: Inuit perceptions', in Freeman (ed.) 1976, vol. 1.

Brody, Hugh, 'Continuity and change: Settlers and Inuit of Labrador', in Brice-Bennett, 1977.

Denendeh. A Dene Celebration, Yellowknife: The Dene Nation, 1984.

Freeman, Milton M. R. (ed.), *Inuit Land Use and Occupancy Project*, Ottawa: Minister of Supply and Services, 1976.

Pitseolak, Peter, *People from Our Side*, Edmonton: Hurtig, 1975.

Richardson, Boyce, *Strangers Devour the Land*, Toronto: Macmillan, 1975.

Riddington, Robin R., *Swan People: A Study of the Dunne-za Prophet Dance*, Ottawa: Mercury Series, National Museum of Man, 1978.

Sidney, Angela, *Tagish Tlaagú. Tagish Stories*, recorded by Julie Cruikshank, Whitehorse: Council for Yukon Indians, 1982.

Smith, Kitty, *Nindal Kwädindür, 'I'm Going To Tell You a Story'*, Whitehorse: Council for Yukon Indians, 1982.

Steltzer, Ulli, *Inuit: The North in Transition*, Vancouver: Douglas and McIntyre, 1982.

2. Other sources

Bliss, L. C. 'North American and Scandinavian tundras and polar deserts', in *Tundra Ecosystems: A Comparative Analysis*, ed. L. C. Bliss, O. W. Heal and J. J. Moore, pp. 8–24, Cambridge: Cambridge University Press, 1981.

Bockstoce, John R. *Whales, Ice, and Men. The History of Whaling in the Western Arctic*, Seattle: University of Washington Press, 1986.

Briggs, Jean, *Never In Anger*, Cambridge, Mass: Harvard University Press, 1970.

Brody, Hugh, *The People's Land*, London: Penguin, 1975.

Brody, Hugh, *Maps and Dreams*, 2nd ed., London: Faber and Faber, 1986.

Buliard, Father Roger P., *Inuk*, London: Macmillan, 1953.

Calder-Marshall, Arthur, *The Innocent Eye. The Life of Robert J. Flaherty*, New York: Harcourt, Brace and World, 1963.

Campbell, Maria, *Breed*, Edmonton: Hurtig, 1969.

Canadian Arctic Resources Committee, 'Brief to the Task Force on Native Claims Policy,' *Northern Perspectives* 13(5):1–13, 1985.

Cooke, A., *The Ungava Venture of the Hudson's Bay Company, 1830–1843*, PhD Dissertation, University of Cambridge, 1969.

Damas, D. (ed.), *Handbook of North American Indians*, vol. 5: *Arctic*, Washington: Smithsonian Institute, 1984.

Dunning, R. W., 'Ethnic relations and the marginal man in Canada', *Human Organization* 18(3), 1959.

Ellis, Henry, *A Voyage to Hudson's Bay . . .*, London: H. Whitridge, 1748.

Fenge, Terry and Joanne Barnaby, 'From recommendations to policy: battling inertia to obtain a land claims policy', *Northern Perspectives* 15(1), 1987.

Hakluyt, Richard, *The Principal Navigations Voyages Traffiques and Discoveries of the English Nation*, vol. 8, Glasgow: James MacLehose and Sons, 1903–5.

Harrington, Richard, *The Face of the Arctic*, New York: Abelard-Schuman, 1952.

Harris, Marvin, 'The 100,000 year hunt', *The Sciences* 26(1), 1986.

Harrison, Julia D., *Métis, People Between Two Worlds*, Vancouver: Glenbow-Alberta Institute and Douglas and McIntyre, 1985.

Helm, J. (ed.), *Handbook of North American Indians*, vol. 6: *Subarctic*, Washington: Smithsonian Institute, 1981.

Lantis, Margaret (ed.), *Eskimo Childhood and Interpersonal Relationship; Nunamiut Biographies and Genealogies*, Seattle: University of Washington Press, 1960.

Mailhot, Jose, 'Beyond everyone's horizon stand the Naskapi', *Ethnohistory* 33(4): 384, 1986.

Mowat, Farley, *People of the Deer*, Boston: Little, Brown, 1951.

Mowat, Farley, *The Desperate People*, Boston: Little, Brown, 1959.

Parry, W. E., *Journals of the First, Second and Third Voyages for the Discovery of a North-West Passage . . .*, London: John Murray, 1828.

Rasmussen, Knud, *Report of the Fifth Thule Expedition 1921–24*, Copenhagen: Gyldendalske Boghandel, Nordisk Forlag, 1930.

Rich, E. E., 'Trade habits and economic motivation among the Indians of North America', *Canadian Journal of Economics and Political Science* 26(1): 35–53, 1962.

Riddington, Robin R., 'The medicine fight: an instrument of political process among the Beaver Indians', *American Anthropologist* 70(6), 1968.

Ross, W. Gillies, *Arctic Whalers, Icy Seas*, Toronto: Irwin Publishing, 1985.

Sahlins, Marshall, 'The original affluent society', in *Stone Age Economics*, London: Tavistock, 1974.

Slobodin, Richard, *Métis of the Mackenzie District*, Ottawa: Canadian Research Centre for Anthropology.

Speck, Frank G., *Naskapi, the Savage Hunters of the Labrador Peninsula*, University of Oklahoma Press, 1935.

Stefansson, Vilhjalmur, *My Life with the Eskimo*, London: Macmillan, 1913.

Stefansson, Vilhjalmur, *Not By Bread Alone*, New York: Macmillan, 1946.

Tatti, Fibbie and Mitsuko Oishi, *Koyere Workbooks (1, 2, etc.)*, Yellowknife: Linguistics Programmes Division, Government of the North west Territories, 1979.

Usher, Peter, *Fur Trade Posts of the Northwest Territories 1870–1890*, Ottawa: Department of Indian and Northern Affairs, 1970.

Usher, Peter, *The Bankslanders: Economy and Ecology of a Frontier Trapping Community* (3 vols), Ottawa: Department of Indian and Northern Affairs, 1971.

Vanstone, James W., *Athapaskan Adaptations*, Arlington, Illinois: AHM, 1974.

Index

Index

253

Index